KNOWING BEING ACTING

A TRANSPERSONAL PSYCHOLOGY INQUIRY INTO THE MEANING OF ACTING
FROM ACTION TO TEXT TO ACTION
A PHENOMENOLOGICAL UNVEILING

JIAWEI LIU, Ph.D.

1 Plus Books

San Francisco 2025

1 Plus Books
http://1plusbooks.com

Author： Jiawei Liu, Ph.D
Title： Knowing Being Acting
Subtitle: A Transpersonal Psychology Inquiry into the Meaning of
Acting from Action to Text to Action, A Phenomenological
Unveiling

2024 1 Plus Books®
Paperback Edition
Published and Printed in the United States of America

ISBN: 978-1-949736-95-3
LIbrary of Congress Control Number: 2025901844

Publisher : Yan Liu
Book Design: 1 Plus Books
Suggested Retail Price : $24.99

San Francisco, USA , 2025
https://1plusbooks.com
email: 1plus@1plusbooks.com

About the Author

Jiawei Liu holds a Bachelor of Arts in Theatre Performance from Shanghai Theatre Academy, a Master of Arts in Theatre Directing from Moscow State University of Arts, a Master of Arts in Multimedia Communications from the Academy of Art University, and a PhD in Transpersonal Psychology from Sofia University. He is the Executive Vice President of Golden Gate College, a Board Member of California Private University, and Chair of the Drama and Psychology Association under the Da Vinci Education Foundation. His published works, including Training Language for Directing and Acting, On the Stage, and Transpersonal Methods in Actor Training, explore the theoretical and practical intersections of acting and psychology. His scholarly contributions, featured in journals such as Art Evaluation and Drama House, reflect a sustained engagement with performance studies and psychological inquiry. Liu's contributions extend beyond scholarship to innovation, holding patents for an Intelligent Sandplay Device and a Dramatic Performance Display System, both exemplifying his commitment to advancing the field. His original theatrical works, such as Moving and The Sage Confucius, further demonstrate his synthesis of psychological insight with creative practice, positioning him as a significant voice in the evolving dialogue between psychology and the performing arts.

Dedication

To my wife Kathy,

*Thou art the pillar of our home, the steadfast heart that bore its
burdens while I journeyed in creation's realm. No words suffice
to measure my gratitude, nor can my pen convey the depth of
thy sacrifice. Thus, I offer thee this book, a humble token of my
boundless love and eternal thanks, for all thou hast done and
all thou art to me.*

Prologue: A Journey to Awaken the Soul

We live in an age of relentless motion, swept along by ceaseless tides, racing from one role to the next, rarely pausing to meet the shadow that silently follows us.

Look closer, dear traveler. Before the mirror, before the scrutinizing eyes of others, we craft an "I"—a mosaic of words, gestures, and expressions. Yet, here lies the riddle: Is this "I" truly who we are, or but an echo of what we wish to appear? What is this body we carry, these emotions we feel, this self that twists and turns under the crushing weight of the world's expectations, endlessly searching for meaning?

Acting, as ancient as the first flickers of human consciousness, is one of humanity's primal forms of expression. Yet, for me, it transcends the boundaries of art; it becomes a portal—a sacred gateway to life itself. Acting is a call to awaken, to reclaim what is real. The actor on the stage does not simply play a role; they embark on a communion with their body, their emotions, their very awareness, and the ethereal space that envelopes them. In this communion, the veils of pretense fall away, revealing the raw bond that connects the self to the world. Acting is no mere mimicry—it is an act of becoming. It is a return to presence, a homecoming to truth, a rediscovery of the essence of being.

This book, Knowing Being Acting, invites you, the reader, to step beyond the curtain and delve into the profound essence of performance. It is not merely a guide for actors; it is an odyssey—a daring quest to transcend the boundaries of selfhood and uncover the untamed, unfiltered heart of existence itself.

Picture this scene: an actor stands alone on the stage, their silhouette illuminated against a boundless void. In this moment, their body is no longer a mere instrument of utility but a vessel brimming with consciousness, a bridge between the tangible and the invisible realms. Each breath is a revelation; each gesture, a symphony. They infuse life into their every movement, melding emotion and action into a seamless, fluid dance. What emerges is not mere performance, but silent poetry—a language that transcends words and speaks directly to the soul.

Strip away the words, and the body begins to sing its primal song. Through motion and stillness, the actor molds unseen emotions into living form, conjuring them from the ether as if summoning spirits into being. This is the primal language of humankind, older than words and deeper than sound. It bypasses the labyrinth of reason and strikes directly at the heart, stirring what has long lain dormant, forgotten, or buried. In the silence of the actor's presence, we confront our own reflections—our fears, our joys, our deepest yearning to feel fully and unapologetically alive.

Performance, at its core, is a celebration of presence. To act is to awaken completely, to feel the rhythm of time and space coursing through the fragile, fleeting now. This profound power of presence transcends the stage; it is the pulse of a life truly lived.

What if you could live in this way? Imagine reclaiming the wisdom of your body, embracing your emotions as they rise and fall, and breaking free from the roles and expectations that confine your spirit. Acting offers us this path. It whispers softly: You are not a machine. Your body breathes with vitality, your emotions carry meaning, and your existence—your very presence—is a gift waiting to be unwrapped, moment by precious moment.

This book is for more than actors. It is a beckoning call to all who yearn to rediscover their true selves, to reconnect with the living world, to strip away the layers of artifice and stand bare before the luminous truth of life.

Imagine now: the lights dimming, the velvet curtain rising. But this stage is not in some distant theater—it is here, in this very moment, woven into the fabric of your life. Every breath you take, every movement you make, is part of the grand performance, reminding you that you are both the actor and the author of your story.

Will you step forward into the light? The world awaits you. The applause swells, already trembling in the air, an echo of the greatness that you are poised to reveal.

Take your rightful place—not as a mere spectator to life but as its star. For life itself is the grandest of stages, and you, the eternal performer, are the miracle it has been longing to behold.

December 17, 2024
Written in my home in Fremont

Abstract

Knowing Being Acting:

A Transpersonal Psychology Inquiry into the Meaning of Acting from Action to Text to Action a Phenomenological Unveiling

by Jiawei Liu, Ph.D.

What is acting? This fundamental question lies at the heart of this book, Knowing Being Acting, explored through the lenses of transpersonal psychology and phenomenology. Drawing on extensive experience in performing and directing theater arts, this work delves into the deeper essence of acting, guided by Husserl's transcendental phenomenology and Ricoeur's existential phenomenology. Ricoeur's theory, with its integration of interpretation in both discourse (dialogue and text) and action, emerges as a particularly meaningful framework, bridging the concepts of "acting" and action in profound ways.

For decades, the field of acting has been heavily influenced by the groundbreaking theories and practices of Stanislavsky. While transformative, these foundational ideas can be further enriched by incorporating concepts from transpersonal psychology—especially those focusing on spirituality, consciousness, transformation, and community. By weaving together these disciplines, this book offers a unique perspective on the multifaceted art of acting, inviting readers to journey through new realms of understanding.

To uncover the profound truths of acting, ten seasoned practitioners—teachers, directors, and actors—were invited into structured conversations, sharing their invaluable insights and lived experiences. These exchanges, carefully transcribed and meticulously analyzed, unraveled a rich tapestry of reflections, offering a window into the heart of the craft. Through the rigorous lens of phenomenological inquiry, the multifaceted nature of acting began to surface, revealing themes as timeless as the stage itself.

Acting, as explored here, is far more than the mere assumption of roles. It is a sacred endeavor where actors, like vessels of human artifice, take on characters not just to perform but to understand—to labor with their very soul in fathoming the depths of another's existence. This pursuit, noble and transcendent, rises beyond the technical domain, becoming an alchemy of experience where the actor's essence and the role's spirit merge as one.

Yet, even in its transcendence, acting is bound by the limits of mortality. No performer, no matter how gifted, escapes the reminder of imperfection—a humbling truth that amplifies the fleeting beauty of artistry. To fully integrate a role into one's lived reality is both an arduous challenge and a sublime act, akin to weaving the threads of life into the fabric of the stage. Great performances arise not merely from talent or the allure of the role but from a harmonious convergence of preparation, spirit, and serendipity. At its core, acting is a triadic relationship—actor, role, and audience. This dynamic connection, like celestial bodies in orbit, ignites the stage with ephemeral brilliance and leaves lasting impressions on both the performer and the viewer.

Through this book, I attempt to demonstrate how transpersonal psychology can enrich the actor's understanding of their craft. Acting, in my view, is not merely an external skill but a deeply transformative experience. By integrating training, interaction, and lived experiences, actors can explore the full spectrum of human emotion—passion, frustration, love, and more—while forming deeper connections with their characters, audiences, and inner selves. This perspective not only elevates the art of acting but also provides valuable insights for drama education. It opens pathways for a more holistic and humanistic approach to teaching performance, inspiring educators to refine curricula that address the evolving needs of performers in a dynamic world.

This book revolves around the central question: What is acting? To delve deeper, I conducted in-depth interviews with ten seasoned professionals, including actors, directors, and educators. Their experiences and reflections, analyzed through the rigorous methodology of phenomenology, reveal the complexity and richness of acting. Acting, as I see it, is a journey of the soul, not merely a performance of skill but a labor of understanding and transformation. Through their craft, actors transcend themselves, entering the essence of another's being. It is an alchemical process where the actor and the character become spiritually intertwined, forging profound connections with audiences and beyond.

While acting can aspire to transcendence, it remains bound by the limitations of human imperfection. No actor, no matter how gifted, escapes the vulnerability of flaws. Yet, it is precisely this imperfection that underscores the fleeting beauty of art. In my research, I explore the ways actors integrate their roles into their lived experience. This process, though arduous, is one of the most remarkable aspects of acting.

Building on Stanislavsky's foundational theories, this book incorporates insights from transpersonal psychology, such as spirituality, consciousness, transformation, and community, to provide a fresh perspective on the art of acting. My goal is to offer actors, educators, and researchers a comprehensive and multifaceted framework for understanding this complex craft. By cultivating deeper awareness of the spiritual, emotional, and psychological dimensions of performance, actors can elevate their craft to new heights. This approach not only transforms acting itself but also holds the potential to enrich education in the performing arts. By inspiring actors and educators to refine curricula and address evolving needs, this synergy of acting and transpersonal psychology paves the way for a more holistic and meaningful approach to theater education.

Knowing Being Acting is more than a blend of theory and practice—it is my reflection on the profound meaning of acting itself. Through the integration of phenomenology and transpersonal psychology, I aim to uncover how acting can embody human experience, spiritual growth, and the search for meaning. My hope is that this book will inspire actors, educators, and researchers to reconsider the essence of acting, while also encouraging readers to reflect on the broader implications of performance in both individual lives and society. This book is not just about the craft of acting; it is an invitation to a dialogue about art, life, and the self.

Acknowledgements

I would like to express my heartfelt gratitude to the remarkable individuals who have supported me during the writing of this book. Special thanks go to Dr. Marilyn Schlitz, Dr. Ted Esser, and Dr. George Guim for their invaluable guidance and wisdom. I am especially grateful to my dear friend, Jet Hermes, Psy.D., for his unwavering support and encouragement throughout the publication of this book.

A very special thank you goes to three extraordinary women who have shown me motherly love and care throughout this journey: my mother, Cao Lin; Dr. Liz Li, President at Golden Gate College; and May Zhong. My mother has been a constant source of strength and inspiration, always encouraging me with her boundless love. Dr. Liz Li has supported me with unparalleled kindness and dedication, especially during my illness and leg surgery, staying by my side with unwavering care and encouragement. May Zhong, with her thoughtful gestures and tireless effort to ensure I was well-fed and cared for, brought comfort and warmth to my life during the book's creation. Their love and selflessness have deeply touched my heart and will always remain a cherished part of this journey.

I am also deeply thankful to my family and friends for their encouragement and belief in me. This book would not have been possible without their collective support.

TABLE OF CONTENTS

Chapter 3: Methods   51

Chapter 4: Results   *73*

Chapter 1: Introduction

It is obvious that conventional wisdom and contemporary acting schools seem to already provide an answer to the question "What is acting?" Additionally, a multitude of literature, including the influential works of Stanislavski (1936/2013, 1957/2014) seek to further answer this question (e.g., Fljiyan, 2008; Wain, 2005). Yet, this question has not been answered from a transpersonal psychology perspective, which has both initiated and encompassed the research of this dissertation. Consequently, this research explores the questions "Who is the actor enacting; the character or the self?" and "Is the performer off the stage still an actor, or a separate person with a separate identity?"

This chapter presents the study's background and provides definitions of transpersonal psychology and its research methods. Also discussed is how transpersonal psychology served as the fundamental theory for this research and was utilized to explore the internal relations between transpersonal psychology and actors' drama in performance. Furthermore, the researcher's background, information about the study's objective and novelty, as well as an introduction to the study's methodology are discussed.

Background

The acting field has been greatly influenced by the theories and practices of Stanislavsky (1936/2013, 1957/2014). Yet, these theories and practices could be enhanced by applying new concepts and practices derived from transpersonal psychology, especially regarding the problematic, if not conflictive, situations that an actor is confronted with when deciding on how to perform a character on stage.

The decision to investigate the meaning of acting from a transpersonal psychology perspective was derived from the researcher's personal experience of directing a play for the Chinese Association in San Jose, California (CA) in 2018, after being traditionally trained in a Chinese acting school. During the professional preparation and rehearsals, the main theme of "What is acting?" remained in this context. An initial survey of the literature revealed typical topics discussing training, skills, techniques, and the issue of actor character, self, and identity. However, in relation to acting and transpersonal psychology little research was found. Thus, participant narratives as variations on the conventional views about acting were used by the researcher to expand and support personal experience and enable the researcher to write a phenomenological description of acting from a transpersonal perspective. This process introduced questions such as:

- How important is technique and training?

- Can the actor-identity be separated from the individual-identity?

- Can stage life be separated from real life?

How can transpersonal psychology contribute to the development of training, skills, and the notion of character and self?

Research Objective and Novelty

In contrast to research done in the natural sciences, inquiries in the human sciences in general, and transpersonal psychology specifically, are not always focused on validating hypotheses that seek confirmation; rather, the novelty of phenomenological research and application of transpersonal psychology to acting lies in the uncovering of meaning. Therefore, this dissertation is not intended to prove a hypothesis. Instead, it aims to (a) investigate to what extent the experience of Chinese practitioners (i.e., actors, directors, and teachers in the field of acting) on the topic correlates with that of the general praxis as described in contemporary literature, and (b) further explores the topic from a transpersonal perspective using the data provided to the researcher by Chinese practitioners. Thus, the objective of this dissertation is to uncover hidden possibilities that could further the praxis in the acting field, by incorporating transpersonal psychology practices into actor training.

Introduction to the Research Method

A detailed description of the method is found in Chapter 3. Here, a brief outline is offered in a manner that highlights an important fact: the needed coincidence of theory and method, something that characterizes phenomenological research and thinking and transcendental constitutive phenomenology and hermeneutical phenomenology. The researcher employed transcendental constitutive phenomenology and hermeneutic phenomenological research methods. This study employed a qualitative hermeneutical phenomenology that studies interpretive structures of experience described from the conversations between the author and the practitioners. A phenomenology is an approach to qualitative research that describes the meaning of a lived experience of a phenomenon for several individuals, which in the case of this study is the experience of acting for different practitioners. The purpose is to describe the commonalities of the acting experience.

A hermeneutical phenomenology focuses on the researcher's interpretations of what lived experience means. This approach views the methodology as a series of logical steps that involve several rounds of reading, writing, and reflexivity in which the researcher is not a passive observer or manipulator of the data, but instead engages in a phenomenological process, accounts for multiple perspectives from participants, and utilizes rigorous data collection and analysis methodology. Again, this study's method is detailed in Chapter 3. First, we must define some of the terms used.

It is essential to define terminology to orient the reader to the researcher's perspective and to acknowledge that there are several types of phenomenology. This study studies the subject (acting) from a transcendental constitutive phenomenology and hermeneutic phenomenology. According to Barua (2009), "transcendental constitutive phenomenology studies how objects are constituted in pure or transcendental consciousness, setting aside questions of any relation to the natural world around us" (p. 4). Additionally, it is important to define what is meant by hermeneutic phenomenology. As Laverty (2003) explained,

Hermeneutic phenomenology is concerned with the life-world or human experience as it is lived. The focus is toward illuminating details and seemingly trivial aspects within experience that may be taken for granted in our lives, with a goal of creating meaning and achieving a sense of understanding. (n.p., para. 12)

The inseparableness of phenomenological inquiry or research from phenomenological writing or textual reflection may involve the visual and auditory languages of images, art, music, or drama. It is an obvious truth that one may find it impossible to locate an underexamined academic area. Though there may still be a need for some modifications and more research, this study makes the academic circle more unique, as it eliminates research gaps. It is the arena of acting or the performing arts that empowered this researcher to contribute to a particular area in which there was a need for more research. Thus, the researcher found it fit to embark on the topic of this dissertation study.

To successfully triumph on this search, many books, articles, and relevant materials were consulted. The work contained in this dissertation employs a phenomenology that cannot be falsified. A method that allows studying and mastering the ineffable dimensions of consciousness with care. Results from the data collection are presented in a phenomenological description of the phenomenon under study, which involves several rounds of reading, writing, and reflexivity in which the researcher is not a passive observer or manipulator of data, but instead engages in a phenomenological process which also fully matches a transpersonal process (i.e., reflexivity that correlates with mindfulness).

Researcher's Background

The author of this dissertation has 15 years of experience in acting and directing. One of his central focuses is the Stanislavski Theater and contemporary acting. He holds a bachelor's degree in Drama Acting from the Shanghai Theater Academy, China; a master's degree in Theater Directing from the Moscow State University of Culture and Arts in Russia; a second master's degree in Multimedia Communications from the Academy of Art University in San Francisco, CA; and was at the time of research, pursuing a Doctor of Philosophy in Transpersonal Psychology at Sofia University in Palo Alto, CA, with a focus on the relationship between drama and psychology.

His professional works include Tutorials of the Language of Drama Acting and Directing published by Xinjiang Art Photography Publishing House, and On the Stage published by Visuals Press. Director credits include Saints Confucius, the original Zhang Guangtian, Flies, the original Sartre; screenwriter and director credits include the drama Moving and At the Playground. He has starred in the plays Paradise Wind Chimes, Gadfly, Resurrection, Original Sin, East House West Room, Thunderstorm, Secret Love Peach Blossom Spring Rainy Summer, Playing Wild Duck, Dream, Hamlet, Othello, Macbeth, Martial Arts. Apart from theater, he is the director of the documentary The Making of Drama, which was published in the 2014 San Francisco International New Concept Film Festival and won the Best Documentary Director award. The researcher will frequently use first-person pronouns throughout the dissertation.

Dissertation Overview

This chapter introduced the research question along with its background to provide an introductory overview of the work to orient the reader. The following chapter reviews relevant literature on the main areas of interest on the topic. Chapter 3 discusses the research methodology, Chapter 4 presents the results organized into seven themes, Chapter 5 discusses the results, and Chapter 6 draws conclusions. The appendices (A–C) include participant recruitment forms (Appendix A invitation letter and Appendix B informed consent) and information on the participants' backgrounds (Appendix C).

Chapter 2: Literature Review

Introduction

Existing relevant literature on the question "what is act-ing?" can be divided into two categories. The first category in-cludes general literature related to theory, training and skills, and the identity of the actor versus the character. The second category looks at publications more specifically linked to act-ing and transpersonal psychology. Also, fields of literature are of primary relevance to this inquiry, the small but burgeoning field of research into transpersonal functioning altogether, and the rather large body of literature surrounding the theory and practice of acting.

Some items placed under the general category may also fall under the transpersonal psychology category due to con-tent overlap; and each categorization is a matter of specific, content orientation and organizational emphasis. In previous-ly published performance research, transpersonal psychology knowledge has not been employed to express emotions and senses reasonably and accurately. However, in this study the re-searcher has put together statements related to explaining act-ing and has come to a new understanding of what acting is. The researcher's understanding is that through of transpersonal psychology research, we can train the performance method of sensory memory. The literature on training, skills, and notions of role's character versus individual identity are intertwined, more so when transpersonal psychology is discussed in a study.

Definitions of Transpersonal Psychology

Transpersonal psychology is the study of transpersonal experiences and behaviors (Myers, 2008). Transpersonal experiences include those actions in which "the sense of identity or self extends beyond (trans) the individual or personal to encompass wider aspects of humankind, life, psyche, and cosmos" (Walsh & Vaughn, 1993, p. 3) and transcend conventional limitations of space and time Transpersonal behaviors include those actions in which existing physiological or behavioral capabilities expand—in the sense of enhancement or opening up, or surpassing in the sense of exceeding, rising above, or going beyond what is ordinarily given or presented in the individual's usual experience of body, self, time, world, and others (Murphy, 1992).

Scholars of transpersonal psychology divided the mind of human beings into three stages: the ex-personal, the personal, and the trans-personal (Walsh & Vaughan, 1993). The individual was the integrity of body, mind, soul, and spirit (Wilber, 2000). It was believed that relations of different levels of the mind were not the stage style but the continuous ancestry, which was like a spectrum (Scotton, 1996). Transpersonal psychology could be regarded as the breakthrough in the development of traditional psychology, as it tried to provide a more inclusive cognitive pattern to broaden the understanding of psychology. The concept also provided the basis for the integration of different schools in psychology with the intention of producing more effects to learn the individual and explore the personality.

At its essence, transpersonal psychology is the study of parapsychological phenomena: "human experiences and behaviors, transformative capacities, and acts of creativity that surpass commonly accepted ideas of basic human limitations to reveal possibilities of action not easily accounted for by traditional psychoanalytic, behaviorist, and humanistic schools of thought" (Cunningham, n.d., p. 8). Studying a range of otherwise inexplicable states of being (including altered states of consciousness), transpersonal psychology helps "bridge science and spirit" (Cunningham, n.d., p. 8) and therefore serves as an apt lens for examining the nature of acting. Understanding the nature and experience of acting is this study's focus. This study seeks to understand how actors describe performing (for example, as an "out of body experience"). According to Cunningham (n.d.), transpersonal psychology research can take on a qualitative, quantitative, or mixed-methods design. The flexibility of method allows the researcher the freedom to study transpersonal experiences and behaviors (p. 8).

Furthermore, transpersonal psychology values the diversity of expressions of human experience while recognizing the universality of its deeper dimensions. Scholars of transpersonal psychology actively seek out and integrate insights on human nature and healing from a wide variety of cultures, taking care to recognize the role of the cultural context in the experience of individuals and groups. Transpersonal psychology requires us to challenge our culturally defined views of mental health and psychotherapy and to draw cross-cultural insights into its practices and applications. But more can and should be done in this area. Scholarship in the field of transpersonal psychology recognizes two responses to the question of diversity. From one perspective, it recognizes and honors the astounding variety of the manifestations of being. The other perspective acknowledges cultural diversity and there is good work on gender, age, sexual orientation, and biodiversity in relation to spirituality.

Traditional Training, Methods, and Techniques for Acting

A definition of acting is offered by Goldstein (2015) as a universal human activity, and one that is uniquely human—no other animals create drama. Further, Goldstein explained acting as a strange phenomenon, but one that we take for granted. For example, actors pretend to be someone else for the audience's enjoyment without intent to deceive. As such, acting is a skill and a form entertainment of public interest. Thus, methods and techniques were developed over time to prepare and develop the actor.

Methods and techniques to master this occupation are presented by different experts of acting, such as Konstantin Stanislavski (1936/2013, 1957/2014), Anne Bogart and Jacques Lecoq (2004), Jerzy Grotowski (2002), and Vsevolod Meyerhold (1978).

These individuals have shaped the concept of acting and assisted in the development of acting training programs.

Stanislavski (1936/2013, 1957/2014) presented the dominant thinking on acting and acting training in the West. Stanislavski claimed to offer the best method, focusing on the psychological aspects of training, but physical and vocal training were also central to Stanislavski's system. Stanislavski's multiple publications described his theories used to train actors and the core of acting pedagogy, known as method acting. His entire system revolved around the nature of learning a job holistically, including the emotional, mental, and actual methods of investigation. His system included skills training with a focus on concentration, trust, certainty, expressiveness, and automation. Many of these skills focus on intentional practice guidance and mental aptitudes gained from the field of athletics. The Stanislavski system was an influential and revolutionary approach to the training of actors, as his methods and techniques brought a naturalist approach to realism in acting (Encyclopedia Britannica, 2016). Stanislavski rejected the extra embellished way of performing and encouraged actors to "*live* on stage … an actor must learn to see, hear, and talk anew on stage as his normal senses were prone to paralysis" (Neff, 2005, p. 60).

There are three important concepts in Stanislavski's (1936/2013) system that constitute the thread linking objectives, actions, and units. First, a concept of the *through line of actions* is developed. The through line is the union of the actor's various objectives in performing a role. It incorporates all other objectives, actions, and units. The second concept is *superob-*

jectives, which refer to each character's overarching objective or goal throughout the entirety of the play. The superobjective propels the through line of action. Identifying the theme is the first step in acting; then the actor can display the through-line of action in front of the audience and presents the underlying theme of the story. In acting training, this step is important to illustrate accurately. Third, the concept *units of actions* is created as the smaller individual goals, objectives, and requirements of a character form a through line of action in a play and can be changed after one or another scene. A character can also face different needs within one scene as he collaborates with other characters. Further, Stanislavski (1936/2013, 1957/2014) discussed four interrelated elements included in training that actors must learn and practice:

> 1. *The given circumstances or situation that actors need to transport themselves to while acting: Practicing is an essential part of the acting, and, at that time, actors imagine themselves in those given circumstances to perform the story in a believable manner. They ensure that if they can imagine something, so can the audiences. As a result of using these tactics, a realistic art is produced instead of artificial over-acting.*

> 2. *The use of imagination by the actor: This can be stimulated and, in this way, can be utilized proficiently. What would an actor do in a particular set of circumstances? The reply can help the actor portray the action efficiently. This is how the "magic" of Stanislavsky assists actors in achiev-*

ing the goals in the acting.

3. Improvisation as a necessity since it stimulates the imagination and allows creativity: This practice helps actors to think deeply, provides clearer insight into the character, immerses themselves in the character, and realistically depicts all the traits of the character's personality.

4. Circles of concentration: Enable the actors to visualize the mental points of their focus and keeps their attention on the required goals and objectives easily. Bogart and Landau (2004) provided a practical guide called The Viewpoint, consisting of different training and devising techniques for creating staging with actors, including: time, space, and vocal aspects to include tempo, duration, kinesthetic response, and repetition; shape, gesture, architecture, spatial relationship, and topography; and pitch, volume, and timbre. The authors believed that one cannot create results, as one can only create conditions in which something might happen. Viewpoint training creates in the actor reasonableness to settle on compositional decisions. The exercise prepares the actors for staging practices and enables one to look at the scene in the studio from two perspectives—the actor's and the director's—simultaneously. This is about how perceptual mindfulness in the learner changes and creates a space for that perceptual figuring out; and how it is to be recognized by the learner and not simply applied unknowingly.

Lecoq's (2001) acting strategy is very compatible with the

principles of embodied cognition, due to the guiding principle of "everything moves." With an increased awareness of the connection between thought, feeling, language, and motion, it prepares the actor to communicate and to be motivated to find the best performance in a creative way.

Another major contribution to acting comes from Grotowski's (2002) significant, further ideas in the specialty of theater, specifically on the concepts of poor theater, montage, holy actor, score, contact, and sign. Grotowski needed a space where the actor and onlooker were constrained to each other's responsiveness and thus used the score of actions as a strategy for the actor where the actor can extemporize. The combination of techniques and improvisation creates a dynamic outcome which is considered exceptional and permits the actor to emerge before the onlooker's eyes from the actor's actions. As an influential theorist who has proposed different acting and training methods, Grotowski (2002) focused on the participation of actors as the substance of performance. He stated that physical and vocal aspects are directly related to the psyche of human beings. Thus, Grotowski's approach offered a heightened experience of the self-forgetting; the more extreme, physically involved, and the authenticity of exhaustion all contribute to a state of changed consciousness where their physical experience is pre-dominant and at the core of their learning within the exercises (Evans, 2009). According to Grotowski (2002), the forms of common "natural" behavior obscure the truth; what is needed is a system of signs which reveals what is behind the mask of common vision. He wrote "that artificial composition not only does not limit the spiritual, but it actually leads to it" (p. 17).

Within the theater, Meyerhold's (1978) experiments in the development of acting lead to the formation of modern international theater. He connected the physical and psychological aspects of acting and considered gestures and movements to be important tools in the expression of a character's feelings and emotions. He introduced many bodily expressions to illustrate particular emotions through gestures. These eurhythmics subsequently became part of acting training. Meyerhold opposed the naturalistic approach to acting and insisted that an actor cannot move from naturalism without an alternative form of training. He assumed the director's aesthetic opportunity would best characterize the composed content of the play; that the director's art is authoritative workmanship, he is not performing craftsmanship. Meyerhold also proposed a connection between the actor and the audience, which was extraordinary and different from that accomplished in the naturalistic theater, where the actor basically emulates life, and the observer has nothing to do except notice. In the theater Meyerhold had in mind, the observer should be a part of the process, effectively using their creative mind to tackle the story performed by the actor.

Embodiment and Actor Versus Character

Literature on the topic of character role versus an actor's personal identity is varied and numerous, as it discusses body movement, bodily experience, and the actor-character issue. For instance, Zarrilli (2004) described methods and technical tools that are resourceful in the understanding of embodiment of actor or performer's work. Zarilli (2004) identified the hypothesis of an actor's body experiences in a performance. Additionally, Zarilli (2001) discussed the impact of knowledge on performance and purpose. Shu (1982) assessed Zarrilli's approach and classified combined techniques of multiple cultures. He also noted Zarrilli's significant knowledge of mindfulness and consciousness in the psychological approach to acting, which includes training in yoga, martial arts, and energy to unite the body and mind.

Also active in shaping actor training, Evans' (2009) book *Movement training for modern actors* recognized the practices of the cultural history of movements for current-day actors. He rediscovered the ritual of movements and connection between a normal body and performing body.

Phenomenology and Hermeneutics

Quinn (1990) delves into the enduring tensions in acting that stem from the actor's public identity, proposing that a semiotic and interpretative lens can disentangle the function of celebrity from the authority it simultaneously commands and threatens. Turner (2012), through a hermeneutic exploration of An Actor Prepares and Theatre of the Oppressed, suggests that their intersections and divergences illuminate new possibilities for reimagining theatre education. Johnston (2007) conceptualizes acting as a "manual philosophy," a practice that reveals profound dimensions of existence and Being, offering glimpses into truths that transcend the boundaries of ordinary experience.

Baleviciute (2010) turns to the cognitive aspects of spectatorship, examining how audiences perceive the process of acting and imbue it with meaning. She argues that the essence of successful audience embodiment lies in an actor's embodied performance—a harmony between body, mind, and emotion that resonates deeply with spectators. Zarrilli (2004), building on a post-Merleau-Pontian phenomenology, contemplates the contemporary actor's body as a site of lived experience, exploring how performance can be theorized as both embodied and transformative.

The practice of phenomenology extends far beyond method; it is a discipline of seeing—of attuning one's vision to the phenomena of lived experience. It broadens the mind, enriches perception, and fosters a profound awareness of both the world and the self. As Qutoshi (2018) eloquently observes, phenomenology engages with the raw immediacy of experience—revealed in gestures, expressions, and behaviors shaped by lived realities. It is an invitation to approach life's complexities with intentional curiosity, to dwell closely with the phenomena under study, and to uncover the deeper truths that inform human experience. For actors, phenomenology offers a path into the labyrinth of performance—a way of unearthing meaning, embodying presence, and capturing the elusive interplay between self and role, reality and artifice.

From the perspective of humanity's developmental trends, theatrical performance remains an influential force that profoundly shapes human life. Its role continues to expand across cultural and societal landscapes. While drama primarily fulfills the human need for spiritual and emotional connection, its historical significance as a form of mass media—especially in times predating newspapers, radio, television, and mobile phones—underscores its broader social functions. Drama is inherently flexible, more intuitive than other art forms such as music and dance, and uniquely capable of presenting a three-dimensional fusion of external voice, visuals, action, expression, and internal emotion. As observed, "dance follows only one principle: the transformation of the body on the ground and in the air." Music, too, holds a supporting role rather than a defining one in this form of expression. In contrast, drama is a multi-faceted construct comprising material and spiritual elements that manifest exclusively in the theatrical space. Text, location, character, voice, costume, lighting, and the presence of an audience coalesce into a singular event—a narrative that is renewed with every performance. Even the nightly repetition of the same play does not detract from its immediacy or the ideological weight it carries as an event rooted in both art and thought.

The theatre stage, therefore, becomes a liminal space—one that bridges the virtual and the real, inviting the audience into an immersive world that mirrors the depths of human experience. By embodying roles, drama expands the breadth of life experiences, awakening the imagination and unlocking creative potential. On stage, transformations of action, thought, and emotion occur simultaneously, offering a dynamic synthesis of life's myriad elements. These transformations touch audiences deeply, fostering self-reflection and emotional resonance. Theatre thus serves as a powerful medium for shaping and refining character, as well as a platform for meaningful interaction with the realities of the world and in an era marked by global diversification, the evolving dynamics of society provide fertile ground for drama's continued growth and reinvention. The interplay of cultural exchange, technological advancement, and shifting social narratives introduces new dimensions to drama creation. This diversification enriches dramatic expression, offering both creators and audiences new forms, methodologies, and pathways for engagement. It is this capacity for renewal and adaptation that ensures the enduring relevance of theatre in human development. In essence, modern drama stands as a testament to humanity's quest for meaning, communication, and connection. It not only reflects the complexity of human experience but also serves as a catalyst for transformation—individual, societal, and cultural—making it a cornerstone of creative expression and collective growth in an ever-changing world.

Mindfulness and Identity

Burgoyne et al. (1999) documented the managing of distress among student actors and their management and noted the "unawareness of the aftermath of acting on students and the process of growth" (p. 169). Their findings yield insights into the acting process and underscore the need for the actor's determination of a character's role. Furthermore, Zarrilli (2007) developed the view that "the actor lives the character's life in order to perform; [it is a] lived-experience on the character's behalf performed by the actor rather than just a roleplay" (p. 638). Seeking to achieve unity of body and mind, and exploring an actor's versus the character's life, In a move towards incorporating mindfulness into performance, Shevtosa (2014) revealed the potential of the performer to lend words and actions to become a doer and looked at the manifestation of mythical bodies and soul to encourage a re-examination of an actor's training and an actor's mindful ability to judge their own work.

Acting and Transpersonal Psychology

Acting concepts and practices went beyond traditional approaches of body, movement, and mental and psychological notions. These were reconsidered from a more spiritual dimension, and more explicitly in terms of concepts such as awareness, consciousness, spirituality, and divine self. Acting is elevated to a philosophy: Johnston (2007) described actors as "manual philosophers" who can reveal the meaning of existence, and performance as an activity may require the engagement of the mind and body *alignment* (p. ii). The connection between the man in the *world* and man on *stage* gives a new perspective on acting, the actor, and identity. Grammatopoulos and Reynolds (2013) explored why people participate in drama and uncovered that getting involved in drama provides individuals with a sense of meaning and a feeling of flexible identity through the experience. Research published by Burgoyne et al. (1999) had already discussed the growth and emotional distress of student actors. In a related topic, Kapsali (2013) identified the cultural effect of tai-chi, yoga, and Feldenkrais on a trainee, and discussed the effectiveness of these practices in terms of social and cultural circumstances that operate in training programs for actors in her article "Re-thinking Actor Training."

Acting Phenomenology

Zarrilli and Thompson extensively discuss acting and its various features. One of the most prominent issues they address is nonverbal acting, which has gained significant traction in contemporary acting practices. The authors analyze works by various scholars and practitioners, examining how these contributions influence different aspects of acting. The discussion below focuses primarily on nonverbal acting and how it has been approached by different scholars. It also briefly explores the impact of perception and intention on the acting process. One of the central works referenced in the book is Samuel Beckett's Acting Without Words I. Beckett himself participated in this performance, collaborating with other actors at the Royal Court Theatre. From this work, it can be inferred that performance without the use of words involves "stripping off" verbal language from the acting process (Beckett, 2010). Zarrilli and his colleagues emphasize that one of the significant benefits of nonverbal acting is its ability to deepen understanding and retention of the performance (Blatner, 1996). In a nonverbal performance, the audience engages all their senses, as opposed to verbal performances, where the voice alone can carry meaning even if the audience is not fully attentive. This multi-sensory engagement fosters a stronger connection between the audience and the performance.

Another key advantage of nonverbal acting, as discussed, is the heightened effort required from the performers to ensure the audience fully grasps the intended message (Blatner, 1996). Unlike conventional acting, where actors may sometimes fall into a comfort zone, nonverbal acting demands their full physical and emotional investment. This necessity to "do all they can" creates a dynamic and immersive performance that resonates powerfully with the audience. Zarrilli and Thompson further highlight two fundamental concepts essential to understanding acting without words. Firstly, the body onstage is not merely a physical body but one that possesses embodied consciousness. The purpose of this "living body-mind" is to adapt and harmonize with the performance environment. As Zarrilli notes, "The first thing to note at this point in my first-person description is that 'the body' onstage is not merely my physical body but instead my lived/living body-mind or my embodied consciousness..." (Zarrilli & Thompson, 2019) and the transformed body—created through this embodied consciousness—operates within a set of expectations shared by both the audience and the performer. Both parties engage in an active cognitive process, interpreting and anticipating the progression of the performance. Zarrilli and Thompson explain,

"During the course of the performance, cumulatively both the actor on stage and the audience experience an ever-shrinking world of potential 'actions'…" (Zarrilli & Thompson, 2019). This mutual engagement in "thinking" and perceiving allows for a rich, evolving dialogue between the performance and its observers. Zarrilli and Thompson provide a profound exploration of nonverbal acting, emphasizing its unique demands on both actors and audiences. By focusing on embodied consciousness and the interactive nature of nonverbal performance, they illuminate its significance as a distinct and impactful form of theatrical expression.

The second play discussing nonverbal performance is "The Water Station" by a Japanese named Ota Shogo. Zarilli discusses the play as using the rich language of silence while neglecting the soul of both the actors and the actors and the audience (Yoo, 2007). To ensure that the intended message is driven home, actors in the play use a slow tempo, allowing the audience enough time to contemplate what they see. "… when they originally devised and developed the performance included "acting in silence, and to make that silence living human time, acting at a very slow tempo" (Zarrilli and Thompson, 2019). Ota argued that her intention in writing a wordless was to help her and other artists explore the drama of silence within people. He further explains that she did not intend to exalt humans to extremely difficult heights in the theatrical field but rather to study silence to the levels it has never been studied before (Yoo, 2007).

Zarilli and Thompson provide that the actor's role in silent plays is to embody and inhabit the pre articulate moments. That is, they are supposed to act comprehensively as if there were no words that were expected to accompany them. According to the book, the actor's task can be related to unconscious communication between them and the natural world.

Perception and Attention

Perception and attention are two crucial aspects discussed by Zarilli and Thompson and their importance to the acting fraternity. Perception is important because it helps parties in a theatre fraternity understand each other (Humphreys et al., 2010). The understanding should be understood as having a mutual benefit to both the audience and the actors. Perception on the side of actors comes in where they need to understand the audience's feelings and desires. This is because acting is audience-centered, and if it does not make the audience happy, it may be regarded as not having achieved its intended purpose. (Echterhoff et al., 2009). The dissatisfaction of the audience, according to the book, can be seen in many forms. One of them is indifference, where the audience seems uninterested in whatever the actors are engaging in. audience can also be noisy to indicate that the performance they are witnessing is not the best version of what they expected. Booing can also be witnessed by the audience, but it does not feature commonly in acting. Thus, the actors need perception skills to understand what could be affecting the audience and subsequently devising methods of countering the same.

On the other hand, the audience needs to utilize perception so that they can understand the hidden meanings that may be presented by a play, especially in nonverbal acting (Beckett, 2010). Attention has an equal purpose in ensuring that both the actors and the audience are at par with each other. Upon the creation of a mutual understanding, the audience understands the intended message, and the same cannot happen without both parties being attentive.

The other important aspect in acting is ethics and which has been captured by Zarilli and Thompson. The other who has commented on ethics as part of acting is O'Neil (2013). He asserts that bringing moral law within the acting fraternity increases the admiration of the performance. This is alongside the personal good that actors enjoy when they act ethically. Nielsen (1996) recognizes that the actors themselves face a balancing dilemma between doing what they feel like doing and what is morally upright. He provides that moral actors should favor what is good for the majority of the audience and that they should not be guided by their inner feelings (Nielsen, 1996)

Influence of acting

According to the literature provided by Zarilli and Thompson, acting is brought up from a particular context and for a particular audience. It is presented in various kinds of narratives that represent a historical or socio-political context. The information carried along these narratives carries the implicit reality to our existence and, therefore, can influence how we think and talk about acting. The acting participants, whether through the stage performance or a representation through literature plays, hold a major role in shaping the society towards a certain theme (McCann, 2011). They are referred to as the vehicles of social change. The actors remind us of the past and the forgotten or give us a glimpse of a probable future through intriguing our imaginations and opinions on a certain topic.

Even in the 21st century, where technological advancement has taken shape, acting is highly recognized and promoted on social media platforms. An unlimited number of individuals can access it through the presentation of short plays or music (Cohen, 2013). This type of acting, which fits the current generation, carries specific themes to be addressed in society. For instance, in the current era, the political-related interests feature more than anything else does, and most of the time, they have led to divisions of the followers involved in political parties' beliefs. At such a stage, acting can be the solution through actors presenting performances using various social outlets emphasizing the importance of peace and collaborative co-existence. To emphasize the theme further, they may use varied stage props that fit in the context. When the public is channeled to re-imagine their decisions of supporting political conflicting due to temporal favors and risking the bigger picture of a nation's stability, they can only seek reconciliation and love amongst each other through the message in the plays. That is the power of acting, and it will always have an impact on society's thinking (Cohen, 2013).

Coordination of emotions with acting

Emotions are the driving forces in the process of acting, which involves and surrounds the idea of creation (Tait, 2017). Zarilli and Thompson agree with this notion of connecting the art of acting to the emotions when they indicated that the actors involved invoke a lot of imagination to the audience. The created imagery activates the inner felt emotions of an individual. The most compatible emotions worth playing include anger, sadness, love, joy, and fear. Basically, they represent the situations surrounding our lives (Tait, 2017). Further, emotions and their biological underpinnings are strong influencers in the process of decision-making, thereby raising the bond between the feelings and the body. Hockenbury & Hockenbury (2010) have further described emotions as the complicated psychological condition that interacts with three unique components: a psychological response, an expressive response, and a subjective experience. Through such emotional acting, the actors can create a mark in the audience while presenting a story or the play. The emotions allow them to relate to their life situations, which is essential in the learning process promoted by the technique of acting.

The actors can further reveal emotions through physical evidence such as crying, blushing, laughing, and other varieties of facial expressions, as noted by Zarilli and Thompson literature. For instance, away from the live performances, when a student has parents who occasionally involve them in domestic violence, such students wear a dull face even in school due to the situation they are exposed to. The actors follow the emotional technique to connect the world of acting with daily life conditions, such as that being experienced by the student (Hockenbury & Hockenbury, 2010). You cannot separate emotions from acting. More so, directors love to use emotions as a tool to create cinematic effects and strategies such as suspense and surprise. It increases the bond between actors and the audience.

The actor's psychophysical process

The actors, being the individuals who present the acting to the audience, collaborate their minds and body for effective performance. The psychophysical technique works in promoting the actor's conscious development. Simply, the ability to recognize the resulting sensory and mental condition with regard to the physical stimuli (Tait, 2017). The technique fights to overcome the distinction between the mind from body, action from analysis, and feeling from the knowledge. This is in the bid to attain the highest capability of creating extreme sensitivity of the physical body towards innovative psychological instincts. When the actor is involved in the action of visualizing through the body, the parameter of "self" becomes out of context, and the personified visualization changes the psycho physicality to be (Tait, 2017). Zarilli literature promotes the system of training by the use of Asian martial arts as well as yoga that increases the level of sensory awareness and the dynamism energy that leads to body and mind becoming one.

The base root of acting is largely on action rather than emotion (Cohen, 2013). The primary idea behind the psychophysical method is that if an actor can monitor their actions in a way that they are fully accounted for in the present situation, then the emotion will find a way of developing themselves. Most of the actors understand that being exposed to certain physical forms leads to an inner experience, which can materialize when they permit themselves to reveal it. In addition, this is not acting on emotion; it is real action. The emotion only manifests as a byproduct of the real action, and it takes a lot of effort for the actor to be receptive to it. Thus. It is with no doubt that; we have to get our body active to understand how the form influences the psychophysical relationship (Cohen, 2013). 80% of human communication is largely performed through physical means (eyes, breath, posture, movements, and gestures). This understanding makes it inevitable for the actors to work on their bodies, which boosts the said physical communication (Cohen, 2013).

The body and the training

For effective performance by an actor, the flexibility of the body is inevitable. Some actions require the body to perform extra fast, while others are maybe friendly and encouraging a slow, manageable pace. Further, most of the time, actors use emotionally challenging props or stage materials that may lead the actor to become static. To avoid such, training is necessary more often. Zarilli encourages this practice when he advocates training the actors using the kalaripayattu, yoga, and tai chi practices to develop the body-mind connection. He emphasizes the idea of stage prowess, which requires a high level of awareness and attentiveness from the performer. The state of "the body becoming all eyes"-such that to create an intuitive consciousness needed for the stage performance. The physical body is the big communicating element of an actor to their audience (Tait, 2017).

Body training, according to Zarilli and Thompson, starts by majoring in creating contemporary actor's interiority. Which is the way the performer discovers, awakes, shapes, understands and deploys "energy," concentration, and feelings to the "issue" of acting (the instincts and the setting of the tasks that entail a particular performance rating designed by specific dramaturgy) (Hockenbury & Hockenbury, 2010). The work of keeping the actor's body active starts with the pre-performative psychophysical exercises to energize the body-mind bond through the use of martial arts (Zarilli, 2005). The physical exercises practically enhance the bond since they are the basis of activation through the building of concentration, circulation of the energy, movement of the breath, and the awakening the body-mind in others, performance environment, and ensemble. The initial stages give a lot of weight to the psychophysical training by applying repetitive exercises and initiating the underlying principles. Then the application of some of the principles happens through structured improvisations. The harmonization of the movement with the breath as well as the uniqueness of the external parameters are put into "play" tied with these basic structures, which commence imitating the "performance" conducted by the actors (Zarilli, 2005).

The actor in the performance

For a good stage performance, the actor must demonstrate excellent techniques and exceptional talent on the stage (Riley & Jo, 1997). The ability to perform uniquely is achieved either all the way from birth or through dedicated moments of training (Zarilli, 2005). Some of the best-expected qualities for an actor to have include charisma –the ability to be appealing, captivating, and delightful to the audience involved. This is because they demonstrate the segments of the real-life individuals who play a major part in creating a positive vibe that is more dramatic and emotional, assisting the actor in fitting in the role perfectly. Secondly, actors deserve to have the best knowledge in understanding human behavior so that they can be able to divulge deep into their scripts and bring out the best and accommodating theme. In addition, the quality of intelligence in combining the information from various aspects and issues of life with the play is an admirable step into creating a stunning performance.

Zarilli and Thompson have campaigned for the aspect of hard work for any actor. Intense exercises and commitment to developing mastery skills are the only way to successful stage performance. It requires energy execution into the role the actor is partaking in since it will assist in creating a strong character in the audience's eyes. The prowess in imagination is the key ability of an actor to take the audience in the imaginative world and connecting them to the real feelings of different situations. The imagery creation creates a deep impact on the emotions of the audience. Finally, the possession of courage can never be over-emphasized. It is a vital behavior necessary in making the actor tough and self-reliant during the performance (Riley & Jo, 1997).

The cross-cultural paradigm of performance

Acting is a wide field that is very compatible and understood by individuals from all cultures. It is not limited to any segment of the population. It employs the actions that enhance in breaking any language, social or cultural barrier (Tomleson & Wolf, 2017). Many schools are adopting the extra-curriculum culture of learning through the use of drama. It enables knowledge capturing and increased cultural sensitivity, too, therefore, becoming an excellent methodology that embraces learning within an authentic setting. It becomes hard to separate the language from the culture, especially for the second language teachers. This is because language learning objectives are not only for the communicating capabilities but also for "humanistically oriented culture content" (Zarilli, 2005). The advantages of teaching culture through acting are that it boosts the development of vital social skills, growth of expressive language abilities, creation of literacy, escalated imaginative play, and creation of imaginaries that boost the comprehension capabilities and thinking skills.

Consequently, various groups from a certain community may purpose to perform on various platforms to promote the richness of that particular community culture. They may do so through demonstrating their food, costumes, and representation of some of their community's rites of passage. The audience falls in love with such demonstrations and connects deeply with people of such origins in order to learn more about them. That is the crucial role of allowing the acting to take the central place in our relationships with others (Tomleson & Wolf, 2017).

Presentational and representational acting

The presentational and the representational acting strategies are contradicting ways of keeping the audience-actor attention (relationship). Presentational acting tends to recognize the presence and the approval of the audience, whether face to face addressing them or indirectly by use of a general attitude (looks, gestures, or language). At the same time, the representational operates with the contrary of that. It fails to recognize the audience and treats them as voyeurs (Engel, 2010). On the other hand, considering the actor-character interrelationship, the kind of performance that utilizes "presentational acting" while dealing with the actor-audience connection is most of the time related to the performer applying the "representational acting" within their actor-character context. Alternatively, the kind of performance that utilizes "representational acting," the performer is always related to the tendency of applying "presentational acting" methodology (Engel, 2010).

In the actor-audience bond, an actor has a significant chance in determining how the relationship is maintained depending on how they handle the audience. In some forms of acting, all the performers may embrace the idea of embracing a similar attitude concerning the audience. For instance, the whole artwork produced by Chekhovian usually entails disregarding the audience until the minute of the curtain call is reached (Chekhov, 2020).In other performances, the actors develop a series of relationships concerning the audience. For instance, in the majority of the Shakespearean dramas, some characters portray direct contact with the audience (platea playing position). In contrast, others act in a way they fail to recognize the audience's presence (Dollimore, 2010). However, most Shakespearean dramas employed a direct, renewed, and often natural contact with the audience from the actor's side.

Significance acting art into our lives

Acting is a basic platform where we learn crucial skills that connect creativity and our daily existence (Kaprow, 2020). It is useful in our everyday life where we apply the skills yonder the stage and screens. To begin with, and as revealed in the Zirilli and Thompson work, physical body language is the key to effective communication. It entails 80% of all the other forms of communication. In fact, body language is the first stage of communicating before the speech is introduced in a person's life (Cohen, 2013). Actor's mind about their posture, movement since they are aware their bodies are communicating tools. Such understanding is essential in real life, employed while giving presentations or when meeting new people; the skill helps create a beautiful first-hand impression. Further, the acting process is fun and stress relieving, which is the biggest necessity to our modern life that is full of adversities (Cohen, 2013).

The process of acting is not about changing to a new person. It is discovering the parallelism in what is seemingly different and then discovering yourself in there (Zirilli, 2005). Actors possess the capability of self-control of their emotions and those of others. They are meeting different people, whether being the audience or a fellow performer and placing themselves in their shoes through emotions. With such skills, these actors are often involved in charity and philanthropy since acting raises the level of empathy while reducing the gap between individuals (Zirilli, 2005). Further, acting is a productive and easy way to navigate how to express your emotions safely that proves a high level of emotional maturity.

Forming a relationship between the participants in the basic goal of acting. It is an essential step (Engel, 2010). The spirit of teamwork and collaboration are inherent portions of acting, regardless of the context of the participants' formation. The actors blend with the confidence to reach out to people, whether for help or to make suggestions on a certain area to renovate their way of acting. Therefore, forming efficient communication and listening skills is essential in retaining a strong bond between the audience, fellow actors, and the directors. Such are exact skills that are translated to our real-life for healthy relationship building among the individuals (Engel, 2010).

Even though acting requires one to build up his body and voice for effective performance, the development of the mind is inevitable (Cohen, 2013). The thinking out of the box, the imagination, the persistent "what if" questions are the mind involving tasks. In addition, such are necessities to improving the conditions we are meeting in our normal lives. The acting triggers the creativity levels while thinking about how to express a certain emotion to the audience. At the same time, the script lines, lyrics, and movements mastering increases the level of the actor memory retention, which is a big bonus to everyone, especially the students who require to master the contents of various subjects. In other words, the art of acting is part of everyone's life. It enables us to create the connection between the inner world (in our minds) and that which is outside (environment) hence improving our comprehension of both worlds (Cohen, 2013).

Character, Self, and Identity

Perceiving an exceptional experience of self is characterized by Jung (2009) as a developmental capacity in which the consciousness of the individual expands beyond the ego-centric to identity with a supreme or spiritual Self in the moment of performance. Ashley Wain (2005) explored in detail the relationships between several formulations that might loosely be included into this category, including Stanislavski's true-I, Grotowski's I-I (2002), and Chekhov's (2003) higher ego and creative individuality. Moss (2006) talked about the sense of self ("Who am I?") as essential for an actor's work. Moreover, Ernest and Ketcham (1992) pointed to "Who am I?" as a spiritual question in many mystical traditions that can lead to awakening to the Supreme Identity, the Divine Self, the root of all characters. Jaspers (1968) described the consciousness of self as complex, consisting of at least four attributes: firstly, the consciousness of self thinks on the awareness of activity. Said another way, the self is a source of energy, a wellspring of action. The second attribute is its contrast and the beyond. The self is defined by differentiation from the non-self, which is all other people, all objects, and the whole outer world. The third aspect of consciousness of self is based on identity. One knows that they remain the same person through time, despite gross physical and mental changes from infancy to old age. Fourthly, consciousness of self rests on several functions which allow some flexibility, but which must operate within narrow limits in order to preserve the person as an integrated whole.

Most actors try to find their ways of performance from their experience. However, consciousness of self is hidden behind the experience, which can be hard to grasp. Where is it? What does it look like? Due to its elusive quality, some experienced actors tend to deny its existence or regard it as an illusion. Maybe the elusiveness is exactly the trait of the self? The self basically can be seen as a subject, but actors usually take the self as an objective. No wonder actors can find it difficult to feel it. That is why the self seems to be both real and elusive. Auden (1976) pointed out the inherent duality: I do not know what the core is, only my subconscious can know itself.

Wilber (2004) stated that this Divine Self is reached when the individual feels the Self without boundary; it is a sense of being able to feel Space as Self. Giannotti (1995) proposed the same process of creating a character's sense of self or identity, which also aids in the developmental process of the actor; the objective of creating complex characters acts to develop a more complex self. He highlighted the ongoing issue in actor training and the professional acting process, of whether one brings oneself to the work or somehow leaves personal matters at the door.

That a transpersonal sense of Self can include knowledge of one's ancestral identity or even past life experiences, is explained by Alli (2009). Another possible way actors can experience supernormal self-sense is described by Murphy (1992) as *transcendent personhood*, where an actor experiences an utterly unique personal self that transcends and unifies in essence with all other unique personal selves.

Wylie-Marques (2003) quoted Suzuki's idea of "effacement of the ego" (p. 83) and the sacrifice of the small self, suggesting that it was necessary for access to the transcendental powers of the spiritual Self. Brook (as cited in Hodge, 2000) also worked towards the possibility that an actor can be "moved beyond ego-driven virtuosity to a kind of psycho-somatic integration that he calls transparency; alive and present in every molecule of their being" (p. 22). In other words, Brook saw that once a small self develops, there are potentially several types or levels of Self to explore.

Identity, Consciousness, and Knowledge

Related to the topic of identity is the concept of consciousness and how the actor knows oneself beyond conventional
approaches. Sarath's (2013) work in jazz, consciousness, and
education provides useful insight. Looking specifically at "creativity and consciousness development," Sarath argued for using critical inquiry to bridge the gaps between identity, consciousness, and knowledge. Citing the work of John Dewey,
Sarath called for a level of self-analysis involving inquiry and
reflection; self-inquiry and reflection are also essential aspects
of improving one's acting ability. Importantly, Sarath argued for
the importance of first-person analysis and reflection in order
to best understand "first-person dimensions of consciousness"
(p. 46). Given the nature of this dissertation study, an understanding of what is acting, this researcher is interested in the
"first-person dimensions of consciousness" as it relates to acting. Therefore, first-person interpretations of acting, conveyed
through conversations, is the primary research method of this
study. However, going further, Sarath (2013) claimed, "Most
unique to the integral framework is first-person, self-mediated
critical engagement. Here, awareness takes recourse, through
meditation, to a realm of consciousness entirely transcendent
of mental activity" (p. 47). At this level of engagement, the actor
could benefit from knowledge of transpersonal psychological
concepts to thereby expand their identity, consciousness, and
knowledge.

Related is the work of Adler (2000), who instructed actors
to constantly study because the ideas of great plays are large

and are often "beyond the boundaries of an individual actor's experience" (p. 81). Adler (2000) further asked actors to "get beyond [their] own precious inner experiences" because "the ideas of the great playwrights are almost always larger than the experiences of even the best actors" (p. 82). Hodge (2000) called this sort of perspective "Adlerian Mysticism," which came to be known as *prodigious cosmopolitan knowledge*. He believed that when encyclopedic knowledge is mixed with high cognitive development (Wilber's vision-logic or higher), an individual can develop what Montuori (1998) called transdisciplinary thinking: taking on patterns of complex thinking that can be seen as a higher developmental stage than normal intellectual capacities (Hodge, 2000).

Alternatively, Bates (1987) suggested there may be a possibility in which actors can have direct access to the experience of different times and places that they have never actually biologically lived, which cannot be explained through scholastic research alone. Murphy (1992) indicated that this extraordinary type of knowledge can include psychic abilities to feel information beyond their personal space inside and immediately surrounding the body. The transpersonal capacity to sense and feel beyond the personal-body space can lead to experiences of telepathy, clairvoyance, empathy, intuition/precognition, and ESP (as described by Murphy & White, 1995). At its height, the work of an actor "involves a kind of divinatory act" (Moon, 2008, p. 57). As expressed by Murphy and White (1995), transcendental knowledge can also be in the form of direct insight or "all at once perception" (p. 555). Da (1991) expressed that, at its extreme, this knowledge meets the divine: a high level of presence and creative response that comes from having a fundamental ignorance about anything whatsoever.

Communication

Literature on transcendental knowledge and consciousness as interrelated with bodily, linguistic, and spiritual communication is led by Ali (2009), who has related how actors communicate inner experiences to an entire room, sometimes filled with thousands of people; sometimes through special pieces of work they communicate with a culture at large in historical events; sometimes they communicate between gods and community. He argued that the highest purpose of an actor is to go directly to spiritual sources, to be initiated into a gnostic spiritual process, and then to share or communicate their findings to a tribe, community, or audience. Brooks (1968) stated that this special communication in actors uses a uniquely theatrical language, and Grotowski (2002) said that it can ascend beyond communication to "communion."

Many theorists have worked with the language of the theater. One of the leading voices is Artaud (1958) who wanted to "make metaphysics out of a spoken language" and "to consider language as incantation" (p. 122). But communication is essentially about connection and sharing meaning between and speaker and listener, an intimate event. This capacity for uniquely intimate communication in actors can sometimes be thought of as a transpersonal experience that Braud and

Anderson (1998) called "maximum personal encounter" (p. 25). This capacity to connect, at its height, is a supernormal and almost shamanic connection with all living things as described by Murphy and White (1995).

In his work, Porter (1996) reported that Stanislavski spoke of this communion as requiring the actor to first develop the capacity to communicate in solitude while in the presence of others. According to Salata (2007) this parallels Grotowski's search for communication intimacy and self-revelation in his work on the "holy actor." Furthermore, Seton (2008) revealed that the combination of authenticity and intimacy (i.e., allowing one's deep intimacy to be seen via performance) is partially due to actor's training themselves to be habitually vulnerable. Suzuki (1986) described this exceptional type of communication (i.e., communication with non-human sentience), including animal, plant, and also subtle beings such as deities, characters, and the deceased. Additionally, he proposed that this supernormal communication can take the form of what is sometimes called in spiritual traditions "direct transmission," which in the theatrical traditions can similarly take place between older actors and younger actors, in a process that Suzuki "the transmission of inheritance" (p. 102).

Aesthetics

There is also literature linking the concept of aesthetics to that of knowledge and awareness. One of the best expressions of supernormal aesthetics comes from Rinpoche (1996), who worked in theater with Worley at the Naropa Institute. He stated,

> *The point of Dharma art is to express through action without any struggle of thoughts and fears, we simply give up aggression, both towards ourselves, that we have to make a special effort to impress people, and towards others, that we can put something over on them. (p. 23)*

He went on to mention that elegance really begins as a state of mind, as "the main point of dharma art is discovering elegance, and that is a question of a state of mind" (Rinpoche, 1996, p. 25).

In relation to "state of mind," Wilber (2007) defined aesthetics as a developmental capacity and further explained that it measures a person's answer to the question, "of all that I'm aware of, what do I find beautiful" (p. 24)? He further claimed that if asked this question over time, the answers always follow a developmental trajectory. Housen (1992) pioneered research that demonstrated that aesthetics was a developmental capacity and can thus presumably reach transcendental levels.

Aesthetics involves the developmental stages of what one sees as beautiful (Wilber, 2007). When seeing with the eye of spirit it is possible for an actor to enter a synchronistic "flow" of artistic choices that are "just right" (Wilber, 2000). Also, since actors perform all manner of character and story, even the most twisted and tragic of human stories can be elevated to what is called "sacralization of the ordinary" (Braud & Anderson, 1998, p. 21). Indeed, this study shares the stories of actors with the ability to see—and thus reveal through aesthetic choice—Divine Beauty even in the most unsympathetic characters. Comparatively, in *To the Actor,* Chekhov (2003) articulated a perspective and approach to working on what he calls *entirety and beauty*. He claimed that "if tragedy is played well, even the most grotesque and horrific human dramas can be elevated to an artistic and awesome beauty" (p. 97). In the same way, Aristotle taught that we want to know because it gives us pleasure in poetry.

Community and Service

In connection with community, which is one of the seven principles of transpersonal psychology, Artaud (1958) stated that great actors in moments of transcendence perform actions consciously in service to a character, script, audience, culture, or even an Ultimate Divine. He referred to an actor's performance as a "spiritual sacrifice." For example, actors performing Joan of Arc as if "burning at the stake, and signaling through the flames" (Artaud, 1958, p. 117), a ritual act of total spiritual transformation. Theater has its roots in sacred Greek rituals and continues to perform a ritual function even to this day (Turner, 2001). Actors literally offer their body and voice as vessels for godly sacrifices. Further, Suzuki (1986) explicitly called for a revised theater space "on which to perform for the gods" (p. 22). These scholars identify the communal and service-oriented nature of acting.

On a subtle level, collective psyche theatrical presentations can enact collective healing. Brecht (1964) elaborated on how the theory and praxis of theater is often overtly aimed at guardianship of the collective social health. As one actor said to another aware of the supernormal service required at the summit of this artistic work: "This thing that we do requires more presence, more generosity, more humility and, frankly, more love than most of us are capable of in our daily lives. It's big. But it's necessary. It's necessary" (Moon, 2008, p. 212).

Starting with Dionysian rites in ancient Greece, many forms of theater have served or been worked on by various deities, imps, daemons, gods, and genies (Moon, 2008). The conscious worship of (or spiritual service involving) a specific deity or god forms are loosely grouped under the umbrella term "deity mysticism" (Wilber, 2007, p. 93).

Service is generally seen in the context of easing suffering in some way, which requires what Zeami saw as an actor's self-cultivation for the sake of compassion (Wylie-Marques, 2003). Decroux (as cited in Leabhart, 2007) was known to command his students to "empty out the apartment so that god could come to live there" (p. 38). In other words, to make space for god's presence. Additionally, Dusa was a major influence in actualizing theater as transpersonal service and was famous as a perceived saint of an actress, who demonstrated a sense of absolute devotion in her work, which she used to glorify God, and through which she revealed God's grace, beauty, and passion (Galliene, 1973).

Conclusion

For decades, psychology has been subject to the paradigm of behaviorism; it has increasingly avoided involving the human mind or subjective categories. With the rise of humanistic psychology in the 1950s and 1960s, the paradigm expanded, emphasizing the study of the inner subjectivity of human experience and culminating in a new field known as ego psychology. However, ego psychology remains constrained to the study of the "me," or the conception of personality and ego. In the 1960s, many psychologists began to argue that while the ego is significant, it cannot represent the "true self" (Stanislavski, 2013/1936, 2014/1957). This realization marked the emergence of transpersonal psychology, a field dedicated to exploring questions beyond ego conception: Who possesses the ego? Who is aware of the "me"? This pursuit of the "true self" transcended earlier paradigms, addressing deeper layers of consciousness and transformation. While resistance from mainstream psychology persists, the call to expand this paradigm continues, as rigid frameworks cannot indefinitely suppress the innate nature of human exploration.

This chapter has reviewed relevant literature at the intersections of acting and transpersonal psychology. The links between existing research in transpersonal psychology and acting contributed to the study's primary research question: "What is acting?" In Chapter 4, the themes emerging from this study will demonstrate how participants' views about acting coalesce, while addressing questions that arise from the collected data.

Concepts central to transpersonal psychology—such as spirituality, self-transformation, and consciousness—align closely with the identified themes (Stanislavski, 1936/2013, 1957/2014). Given that transpersonal psychology explores the depths of human psychology to facilitate healthy development in social life, the data collected in this study were analyzed in connection with transpersonal psychology literature. In this research, the focus is specifically on the human psychological activities inherent in the art of acting, as shared and developed by the study participants. The following chapter, Chapter 3, outlines the data collection methods employed for this dissertation's primary research.

The above discussion reveals that acting is inseparable from our lives; it is an art that permeates our daily existence, often performed unconsciously. At its core, acting largely involves nonverbal communication, which constitutes approximately 80% of human interaction. Remarkably, body language serves as our first form of communication before the development of speech in early childhood. In this sense, acting is a phenomenon we are born with, a natural expression that helps us navigate relationships and interactions, much like an actor builds a connection with their audience. Moreover, the phenomenology of acting contributes to fostering ethical values and instilling the morals necessary for maintaining healthy relationships within society.

Acting plays a pivotal role in shaping our existence by celebrating and preserving the beauty of diverse cultural expressions. Through performances, appreciation grows for the

distinctive elements of various cultures, strengthening connections among communities. The emotions conveyed by actors
enable audiences to relate to real-world situations and connect with a range of human experiences and feelings. However,
achieving this level of connection requires seamless collaboration between the mind and body, a process known as psychophysical integration. Constant physical training is essential for
enhancing this mind-body coordination, which, in turn, culti-
vates vital skills such as creativity, discipline, and self-control.
These skills are not limited to the stage but are directly applicable to our daily lives, where the art of acting continues to
influence our behavior and interactions.

The links between acting and transpersonal psychology
are particularly profound. Transpersonal psychology explores
spirituality, self-transformation, and consciousness—concepts
that resonate strongly with the nature of acting as an art form.
Actors, through their craft, seek to transcend the limitations of
ego and identity, tapping into deeper layers of self-awareness
and emotional truth. Acting becomes a journey of transformation, not only for the performer but also for the audience, as it
fosters empathy, imagination, and introspection.

Individuals who engage in acting are often more adaptable
and relatable, as they can adjust their emotional states to suit
different situations. They are also more likely to contribute
to their communities through charitable initiatives, as their
deep understanding of human experience fosters empathy and
compassion. Acting allows individuals to step into another person's shoes, providing a profound sense of what it means to be

someone else.

Given the significant benefits of acting for personal and societal development, policies that integrate acting programs into educational institutions should be prioritized. Such initiatives would nurture creativity, emotional intelligence, and social awareness, equipping individuals with skills that not only enhance their artistic abilities but also enrich their everyday lives.

Chapter 3: Methods

Introduction

This chapter encompasses (a) the philosophical aspects of the phenomenological research approach, (b) Moustakas's (1994) version of the phenomenological research method with its specific procedural steps, (c) the data collection technique (conversations), and (d) the data analysis method (textual descriptions and several rounds of reflexivity). The research presented in this work is best addressed using a phenomenological research approach as described in Creswell (2007). Within this general approach, the researcher chose a specific set of procedures as suggested by Moustakas (1994). This approach and set of research procedures are fully compatible with the Intuitive Inquiry approach for transpersonal research methods suggested by Anderson and Braud (2011), and thus, is both appropriate and complementary of the transpersonal research orientation of this dissertation.

The overall aim of the phenomenological method is to gather information on several individuals about their lived experiences of a concept or phenomenon under study in order to find a common meaning for those experiences. The researcher, through the process of reducing the individual meanings into a description of the universal essence, aims to grasp the very nature of the thing. Below is a description of the philosophical aspects and the procedural steps of the phenomenological research methods used in this dissertation. In the end, this study should give the reader the confidence to proclaim, "I now understand what the experience of acting is!"

Philosophical Background of the Phenomenological Research Approach

Husserl's (1900/2001) original description of his (transcendental) theory on phenomenology was abstract and theoretical. Over time, Husserlian phenomenology branched out into more concrete research more related to studying the life world (i.e., "existential" phenomenology). Such study resulted in developments in both conceptual frameworks and methodological rules thereby generating practical applications for studying phenomena in different fields of the human sciences.

In psychology, Stewart and Mickunas (1990), and many others (Colaizzi, 1978; Giorgi, 1985, 2006; Van Kaam, 1966; & van Manen 2014), developed different procedural ways to conduct phenomenological inquiries, but they all shared a common ground of studying the lived experience; these lived experiences are conscious ones, and the researcher is focused on the description (not explanations) of the essence of a phenomenon. Broadly speaking, practitioners in psychological emphasize four philosophical perspectives in phenomenology, which are intimately connected to the philosophical aspect of transpersonal psychology:

1. A return to the traditional task of philosophy (i.e., a search for wisdom) lost to "scientism" of 19th century philosophy (the scientific method and dogmatic, reductionistic point of views about human mentality, which focused only on behaviors thereby omitting the human experience as a whole) for the natural sciences. Modern transpersonal psychology is a uniquely American psychology and a reflection of America's visionary "folk psychology" and "alternative reality tradition." Modern transpersonal psychology emerged out of humanistic psychology in the late 1960s, calling attention to possibilities of growth and development beyond self-actualization (Gilbert, 2008; Powell & Gilbert, 2007).

2. Suspension of the "natural attitude" and adoption of a "phenomenological attitude" where the researcher suspends any prior (personal) assumptions ("epoche") regarding the phenomenon.

3. Dual Consciousness is always directed toward an object: there is no consciousness without something (phenomenon) to be conscious about. This parallels the concept of "mindfulness" in transpersonal psychology. Thus, an object is inextricably related to one's consciousness of it. Consciousness allows "noema" (the thing as it appears to the experiencer) and "noesis" (the mental context of the experiencer in relation to the noema) to be in a correlational rather than in a subject-object dichoto-

mous relation to each other.

4. An individual writing a phenomenology must include a discussion about the philosophical presuppositions of phenomenology along with the methods and explain that merely following the methodological steps of the phenomenological research method is meaningless unless one adopts the phenomenological attitude (philosophical presuppositions) encapsulated in the concept of reflexivity.

Philosophical Presuppositions Concerning Phenomenological Inquiry

It is very important to stress that in a genuine phenomenological inquiry, it is not sufficient to follow the procedural steps (e.g., Moustakas's (1994) procedural steps as described below) for gathering data (which, in the case of this study is conversations with actors after performances) and creating categories of statements or creating themes from the data. According to Ihde (1986), phenomenology is done by the individual researcher's *engagement* because it is in the "reflexivity" (not mere "reflection") of the individual that the phenomenological inquiry reaches its culmination. That is, if the researcher does not know phenomenology, even if they follow the research steps (Brecht, 1964), the results are "meaningless," or no better than any obtained by non henomenological approaches. Phenomenology is both a *way of seeing the world* and a *methodology* at the same time. That is what distinguishes phenomenology as a "radical" way of knowing. It is not a method to see oneself or the world, or even oneself *in* the world, but rather, it is an approach that involves, better yet, engages one as *"being-in-the-world."*

In terms of this dissertation's topic, only as "being-in-the-world" can one come to an understanding of what acting is from a phenomenological standpoint. Regardless of the phenomenological method used, the resulting methodological process must observe the four operational rules of inquiry:

1. Epoche: Suspend all initial personal assumptions (bracketing).

2. Reduction: description, not explanation (in terms of theories, etc.).

3. Horizontalization: Generate variations from different perspectives.

4. Structural Essence or Invariant: The ultimate goal is to arrive at the "essence" of the phenomenon.

Procedural Research Steps Using Moustakas's Method

Moustakas (1994) translated the previously posed four operational rules into his particular set of procedural research steps. This dissertation follows Moustakas's phenomenological research method, the general description of which is as follows:

1. Determine if the research problem is best examined using a phenomenological approach.

2. Choose a phenomenon of interest to study.

3. Specify broad philosophical assumptions of phenomenology.

4. Collect data. For this dissertation, the preferred data collection method is the use of conversations or interviews.

5. Do a phenomenological analysis of the data, in four activities:

   - Extract significant statements (every statement/variation is given equal "weight," i.e., horizontalization).

   - Group statements into clusters of meaning or themes.

   - Write textural description (what participants experienced) and structural description (context of experience).

6. After several rounds of "reflexivity," the researcher writes a composite description (a blend of textural and structural descriptions) that presents the "essence" of the phenomenon (the essential, invariant structure) to allow a reader to say, "I understand what it is like for someone to experience that." At this juncture, the researcher may reincorporate his own experiences and contexts, and anything of relevance that was previously bracketed.

Transcendental Phenomenological Considerations

As explained by Ihde (1984, pp. 134-139), Husserl's original theory and its strands of phenomenological inquiries involve a process that contains four operational rules or procedures: (1) bracket (describe, do not explain; that is, set aside all "non-essential" considerations; (2) reduce (as one keeps bracketing, additional layers (variations) of the onion are peeled in the effort to get to the core); (3) horizontalization (do not try to give some variations a higher value: no single variation is better than the rest); (4) seek the structural or invariant features of the phenomenon (figure out the essence of the phenomenon). Notice that each of the four phenomenological procedural rules (of doing) have an inseparable hermeneutic counterpart that consists in the element, or better, the process of interpretation. This is recognized by Anderson (2011, p. 28) in her Intuitive Approach to transpersonal research where she notes that hermeneutics is involved in each of the five cycles of the (otherwise conventional, linear) research process. In turn, this points to Ricoeur's (and other thinkers') observation that hermeneutics and phenomenology are dialectically related, and that Husserl's transcendental phenomenology failed to grasp all the consequences of this connection:

"Husserl perceived the coincidence of intuition and explanation, although he failed to draw all its consequences. All phenomenology is an explication of evidence and an evidence of explication. An evidence that is explicated, an explication that unfolds evidence: such is the phenomenological experience. It is in this sense that phenomenology can be realized only as hermeneutics" [emphasis added] (Ricoeur, 1991, p.52).

Van Manen's Phenomenology of Professions

Husserl's transcendental phenomenology is a philosophical theory. He did not provide a concrete methodological guideline for its application because he was coming from a philosophical perspective of a universal concept. Nor did it anticipate the emergence of the existential phenomenologists and its subsequent strands, or the methodological varieties that would be arising from the need to suit different fields of study (psychology, sociology, medicine, the arts, education, etc.) that were applying phenomenology to their specific needs and goals. For the purpose of this dissertation, it is important to mention Ricouer (1991) and his critical hermeneutics of the text, and van Manen's (2014) phenomenology of practice, because their concepts and procedures are used in the inquiry's data gathering and analysis the research question.

Ricoeur's Theory of Text-Reading, Action, and Interpretation

The writing of any text must consider the four traits of language as presented by Ricoeur (1991) in Chapter 7 of *From Text to Action*. See Ricoeur's Text and Action Theory in Section 3 Methodology, under Theoretical Framework in Section 3.

Herda's Conversations vs. Interviews

Also, because of her special understanding of hermeneutics, Herda (1999) makes a clear distinction between a conversation and an interview, something that is not clear even to most researchers using phenomenological methods, it is important to understand how the language to talk about research can completely affect the research itself.

"What is acting?" is a question that has practical relevance for theater and, thus, a *practical* methodological approach is used, following Max van Manen's Chapter 7 on Phenomenology and the Professions, in his *Phenomenology of practice* for the professions (2014).

Van Manen: Phenomenological Reflection and Writing

In this dissertation, its author, researcher, will answer the question of what acting is by collecting data from several performers in the form of conversations, which will be transcribed, analyzed, and turned into a preliminary text for further phenomenological reflection on the text to generate a final description of the phenomenon under investigation. With regard to the writing of this text by the researcher, writing is also not something *appended* to the research. Van Manen (2014, p. 389) highlights that it is "critical to insist on the inseparableness of phenomenological inquiry ... from *phenomenological* writing or textual reflection" [italics added]; and in From Text to Action, Ricoeur (1991) tells us that reading is not so much something we do *to* the text but something the text does to us. Writing and reading *are* the research in the analysis and reflective phases of phenomenological inquiry.

The pre-reflective data of human sciences research are

human *experiences*. Van Manen (2014, p.314) refers to them as the *lived-experience descriptions* (LED) which form the pool of phenomenological variations in which each is one part of the whole, and the whole is more than a mere sum of the parts. The performers are participants in the research project; they provide descriptions of their experience (conversations to be transcribed) but, in this particular case, do not go beyond that through the full phenomenological process. Only the research-er is doing the complete phenomenological research in this particular case because he will perform the phenomenological analysis of the pre-reflective data, reflect and write on it, and do the final writing of the description of the phenomenon.

Ricoeur's theory provides the support for why it is appro-priate to go from "action to text" and then from "text to action:" from the pre-reflective action to a rendering of the conversa-tions into a text of what was experienced, to reading the text and extracting insights that will eventually make the totality of the phenomenon visible and comprehensible and, therefore, enable the possibilities of new ways of "enacting" under new contexts.

This relationship between parts and whole in the text, ap-plied to understanding a text in its totality, presents the re-searcher with the problem of hermeneutic interpretation that Ricoeur (1991, p.159) characterizes as caused by the "very nature of the verbal intention of the text … something more than the sum of the individual meanings of the individual sentences."

Once the researcher has achieved a textural composition, then another cycle of interpretation takes place at the reflective stage and, finally, at the final description stage when an explanation of the essence (structural or invariant features) of the phenomenon emerges. It is important to note that "phenomenological reflection cannot be separated from phenomenological writing, or, better, phenomenological reflection *is* writing" (van Manen p. 365).

Access to these data (human experience) will be indirectly done through procedures akin to Herda's (1991, p. 96-100) hermeneutic field inquiry process which uses critical hermeneutic participatory research *conversations*. A similar procedure for psychology is recommended by Colaizzi (1973) as a series of ten steps in phenomenological research process, as reported by Spinelli (2005, pp.136-137) and involving *interviews*. One important observation is that one must not confuse interviews with conversations. It might seem to be just a matter of semantics but it is not: language generates realities. Heidegger wrote that "language is the house of being." If we keep referring to it as interview, then it will be conceived as a mere interview (one way street, not a two way conversation). A true researcher is not an interviewer, at least not in a phenomenological inquiry proper.

"Knowing how to do hermeneutic participatory research does not mean knowing how to use particular techniques to design questions, create response sheets, and collect and analyze data. Rather, it means learning about language, listening, and understanding. Specifically, it entails an awareness of the critical difference between research that uses tools and techniques [e.g., interviews] and research that lives in language. ....

[t]he charge is more inclusive --- [the goal of language/conversations is] to disclose a world of our participants and ourselves (Herda, 1999, p. 93).

While it is true that the researcher is the one undergoing the full phenomenological experience and is in full charge of the research, it is a mistake to relate to the participants as if it was an interview. The correct attitude is reflected in the very type of questions asked of the participants: they must be phenomenologically congruent type of questions, and these types of questions are not of the types asked in interviews. In a participatory research conversation of the phenomenological type, what researcher and participants have to say to each other, act as mutually-triggering messages that, in turn lead to further mutually-triggering interactions. This is how they mutually *transcend* each other, in the new relation to each other, capable of creating new meanings for the researcher to take into consideration. Even in the writing process the researcher is in a relationship the text, a quasi-person who is *conversing* with the researcher. "Research does not merely involve writing: research is the work of writing" (van Manen, 2014, p. 364) and reading.

The Transpersonal Psychology Method

Anderson (2011) presents her intuitive inquiry approach with five research cycles that match the conventional research steps: Cycle 1 (topic selection), Cycle 2 (literature review), Cycle 3 (data collection, analysis, & findings), Cycle 4 (results), and

Cycle 5 (discussion and implications). They also roughly match the five phenomenological rules of inquiry. See Figure 1 and 2 below.

Figure 1 Phenomenology's Rules of Inquiry

Rule 1: Epoch

Rule 2: Reduction

Rule 3: Horizontalization

Rule 4: Seek structural or invariant features

Rule 5: Write the report on the essence of the phenomenon

Figure 1.2 Intuitive Inquiry. Five Cycles of Interpretation, Each Involving Hermeneutics

Cycle 1:

Topic Clarified via Imaginal Dialogue

Cycle 2:

Preliminary Lenses via Engagement with Literature

Cycle 3:

Data Collection, Analysis, & Descriptive Findings

Cycle 4:

Researcher's Final Interpretive Lenses

Cycle 5:

Discussion of Final Lenses/ Theoretical Implications

Research Process: Procedural Research Steps

On the procedural/operational level of the research design, several guidelines can be found. Among them, Colaizzi's ten step, and Herda's 36 step procedure, listed below.

Colaizzi's Ten Step in Phenomenological Research

Step 1:

Researcher designs brief statement or research question to specify the focus of investigation and to select appropriate conversation partners who are qualified (via their experience) to engage in a descriptively-focused enquiry. This step requires the researcher to engage in preliminary process of self-investigation designed to expose his presuppositions regarding the phenomenon to be explored so that these can be "bracketed" insofar as they are not inadvertently embedded within the starting statement or research question.

Step 2:

The researcher engages in a structured, focused enquiry with each conversation partner. Typically, a one-on-one conversation lasting approximately 10-15 minutes each.

Step 3:

The conversations are transcribed word-for-word. Clearly identify who is talking. For example:

John: I was 10 years old when I had an accident.

Mary: Oh. What happened?

John: I was rear-ended by a drunk driver.

Omit repetitive use of "Uh," "you know," "I mean," etc. when you talk. Do not record those words in the transcripts, unless it is important to show, for example, that the person was nervous or forgetful, and keeps saying "uh, uh, uh…"

Remember: Each minute of conversation will take about 3 minutes to transcribe.

Step 4:

The researcher reads each of the transcribed conversations ("protocols") several times in order to gain a "feel" for their content.

Step 5:

The researcher returns to each individual protocol and extracts those phrases and sentences that directly pertain to the investigated phenomenon so that by the end of this step the researcher has collected a list of significant statements from each protocol.

Step 6:

The researcher seeks to extract or spell out the meanings contained in each significant statement. This formulation of meanings, or movement from what is said to what is meant, is the most precarious interpretative part of the phenomenological research process and requires the researcher's creative insight to both remain true to the conversation partner's statement while at the same time seeking to draw out of it its embedded, often implicit, meaning.

Step 7:

Having formulated meanings from all of the significant statements derived from all of the protocols, the researcher now organizes the aggregate formulated meanings into clusters of themes that may be shared by one, some or all of the conversation partners. The themes may well be contradictory or even unrelated to one another and require the researcher's tolerance for ambiguity. Further, there may be formulated meanings that do not fall into cluster of themes in that they stand alone. These too are added to the final list of thematic elements.

Step 8:

The list of thematic elements is integrated into an exhaustive description of the investigated phenomenon.

Step 9:

The researcher returns to each conversation partner with the exhaustive description so that the partners can respond to it in terms of verifiability as a statement that captures the experiential structure under investigation.

Step 10:

On the basis of the partners' comments, amendments, corrections, novel additions, if any, [after reviewing everything one more time,] the researcher produces a further, usually final, exhaustive description of the phenomenon. While never fully completed, in that the validation attempt will seek on-going refinement for any avowedly "final" statement, nonetheless this step most frequently paves the way for further, and hopefully more adequate research in the future.

At the very least, it allows the researcher to go back to the original statement and to examine how well or poorly it reflected the co-researchers (partners) actual statements, what previously unforeseen assumptions may have either remained within it or was left out that may be significant for future research.

Roughly speaking, Step 1 belongs in Anderson's Cycle 1 (topic clarifies via imaginal dialogue) of the research process. Cycle 2 (preliminary lenses via engagement with literature) is associated with the literature review, not mentioned explicitly in Colaizzi's ten steps. Steps 2-5 belong in Cycle 3 (data collection, analysis, and descriptive findings). Steps 6-8 belong in Cycl4 4 (Researcher's final interpretive lenses). And Steps 9-10 belong in Cycle 5 (discussion of final lenses & theoretical implications.

Herda's 36 Steps in Hermeneutic Field Inquiry Process

Herda offers a more detailed breakdown of the steps in the research process.

1. Make a commitment to field inquiry in a hermeneutic tradition.

2. Choose a topic or research focus carefully.

3. Carry out a review of literature and develop a theoretical framework (the background for the analysis of the conversations).

4. Develop initial categories.

5. Propose initial questions and conversation guidelines.

6. Pilot the questions and conversation guidelines.

7. Select participants and develop entrée.

8. Data collection and text creation.

9. Data analysis

10. Pull out significant statements, develop themes, and place them within categories.

11. Substantiate the themes or important ideas with quotes from the transcripts or with observational data from the researcher's log.

12. Examine the themes to determine what they mean in light of the theoretical framework of critical hermeneutics.

13. Provide opportunities for continuous discussions and conversations with participants using the developing text when appropriate.

14. Set a context for the written discussion.

15. Discuss the research problem at a theoretical level, thus implementing a further practical use for critical hermeneutics.

16. Ferret out implications from the written discussion that provide insight and new direction for the issue or problem under investigation.

17. Bring out those aspects of the study that merit further study.

18. Give examples of learning experiences and fusion of horizons on the part of participants that took place during the research process. Relate the study to yourself in terms of what you learned and what role the study played in your life. Ricoeur's concept of enlarged self can be exemplified with illustrations from the researcher's own experiences.

19. Make a commitment to field inquiry in a hermeneutic tradition.

20. Choose a topic or research focus carefully.

21. Carry out a review of literature and develop a theoretical framework (the background for the analysis of the conversations).

22. Develop initial categories.

23. Propose initial questions and conversation guidelines.

24. Pilot the questions and conversation guidelines.

25. Select participants and develop entrée.

26. Data collection and text creation.

27. Data analysis

28. Pull out significant statements, develop themes, and

place them within categories.

29. Substantiate the themes or important ideas with quotes from the transcripts or with observational data from the researcher's log.

30. Examine the themes to determine what they mean in light of the theoretical framework of critical hermeneutics.

31. Provide opportunities for continuous discussions and conversations with participants using the developing text when appropriate.

32. Set a context for the written discussion.

33. Discuss the research problem at a theoretical level, thus implementing a further practical use for critical hermeneutics.

34. Ferret out implications from the written discussion that provide insight and new direction for the issue or problem under investigation.

35. Bring out those aspects of the study that merit further study.

36. Give examples of learning experiences and fusion of horizons on the part of participants that took place during the research process. Relate the study to yourself in terms of what you learned and what role the study played in your life. Ricoeur's concept of enlarged self can be exemplified with illustrations from the researcher's own experiences.

Data Collection

Data was collected in response to the original research question "What is acting?" The researcher sent a letter of invitation (Appendix A) along with a copy of the conversation questions, to 10 participants who fit the study criteria (as explained below). Individuals who responded to the invitation letter were sent the informed consent document (see Appendix B). Ten participants signed and returned the informed consent document. Data was gathered via conversations conducted over phone or Zoom video chats. All conversations were recorded. Each audio recording was then transcribed. Written transcriptions of the recordings were then translated from Chinese to English.

Data Analysis

Starting from the conversation transcripts, the researcher first extracted significant statements and, in the next step, grouped them into themes that were analyzed and synthesized as results and conclusions.

The first round of results was the reduction of the nine themes into five categories of description. In the second round, these five categories underwent further reflexivity (this time from a transpersonal psychology framework) which, in turn, produced the final description of the phenomenon. At the end, analysis generated seven main themes and 28 subthemes all described in Chapter 4.

Participants

The conversation participants were selected from practitioners skilled in Chinese acting who are actively performing in China or in the United States. Ten conversation participants were selected. These participants were selected for their accomplishments in the areas of theater, movie, or TV performance. Participants were first sent a Letter of Invitation (Appendix A) and the Informed Consent (Appendix B) form that they were asked to read and sign. In addition, participants were asked to make an appointment for the conversation. Sample questions about possible conversation topics were included in the Letter of Invitation (Appendix A).

Conclusion

This chapter presented the research method and the various methodologies used in the dissertation study, which occurred during data collection (conversations with 10 Chinese performers) and analysis. Chapter 4 presents the research results through the examination of themes and subsequent subthemes.

Chapter 4: Results

Introduction

This chapter presents the research results obtained from the significant statements derived from analysis of the collected data (written transcripts of the conversations held with study participants). Then there will be a discussion on the relationship between acting and transpersonal psychology. A total of seven themes and 28 subthemes are presented.

In phenomenological analysis, it is required that we apply the reduction and reflexivity process repeatedly to gain an understanding and describe the phenomenon under study. The result is a description of the essential meaning of said phenomenon. Thus, significant statements were grouped into themes (seven) by the researcher. The procedure used to generate themes followed Giorgi's (1975) proposed phenomenological methodology. The researcher later segregated the themes into two groups. Since participants were unfamiliar with transpersonal psychology, the results presented in this chapter constitute the "objective" and raw data (participants' exact words/experiences). Additionally, the researcher examines participants' more novel or progressive views about acting, but without exhibiting specific concepts from transpersonal psychology.

A discussion of the results follows. The discussion takes the results, already a first interpretation of the participants' views, and further interprets them more the researcher's perspective (knowledge and experience) within an explicit transpersonal psychology framework.

It is in the discussion that the final expression of reflexivity happens and, in accordance with the intuitive approach (method) of transpersonal psychology itself, the researcher will take the themes and think about them producing a new text, drawing on insights, experiences, meditation, mindfulness, and spiritual-level reflection, among other things. The (final) discussion is actually the end of several iterations of transpersonal process where the researcher's own thinking and actualization transcends the originally obtained participants' views, and thus, generate the final phenomenological description of a transpersonal psychology answer to the question of "what is acting?" Since transpersonal psychology is the framework through which acting is being studied, the data analysis process generated a significant number of transpersonal and philosophical thoughts beyond the original research question. Some of which included: How important are technique and training; can the actor-identity be separated from the individual-identity; and can stage-life be separated from real-life?

Researcher's Commentary

There is a personal process that I, as the researcher, want to explain. I conducted the data analysis process several times when a new group of ideas or themes came up, which were not part of the significant statements. Also, I sometimes consolidated and merged two groups of statements in different ways into different groups. After consolidating or merging, it took me several rounds of reflection and many weeks to read the themes carefully and to analyze both the themes and the content. Additionally, I started taking notes in terms of the results of synthesis on the key concepts and ideas related to the research questions. Even though the results may be clear, the way I gained clarity was not simple. It was not necessarily a linear process because it was not a one-time process. Instead, it was a recursive ramification of thoughts, ideas, writing, re-writing, reading, and re-reading between ideas in the transcript and what was extracted in significant statements, as well as the themes and additional notes that I took every time I read the themes.

For weeks I reviewed the collected data—the transcripts, the statements, the themes, rereading, writing, rewriting, thinking, rethinking, adding new themes or consolidating themes or ideas, all in light of the research question—until the conclusions became clear and concise. The following sections portray the researcher's voice leading the discussion with support from the participants' voices. In this level of deeper discussion, I, the researcher, following the themes, move the text discussion with support from the ideas, thoughts, and experiences drawn from the participants' conversations and the researcher's own reflexivity.

Participants

In this section, the 10 interviewed participants' views and summaries are shared (see Appendix C for participants' backgrounds).

Ren Chengwei, an actor, says that the research studies are psychology, the good or bad of the role completion, is highly relevant to the psychological expression correct, accurate, and rich. He also says that those rich in acting are those that know what they want. As Li Jiahang (actor) said, interpreting people or understanding better and deeper about life is attained from having a long-acting experience. He also suggested that acting mostly needs understanding and empathy.

Lei Guohua, a director, said an actor needn't care too much about how they are now, but about they should care about their pursuit in your own hearts and suggests the more experience, the better. He also thought that personality could cost career advancement and says personality made him who he is today. Lin Hong Tong suggested that honing exercising, practice makes perfect, skillful, refined, and strives for perfection. Honing makes me more focused and take life seriously. According to another participant, performing basic teaching is especially bad for children. Li Yike, an actor, suggested "children are born to believe because they have little knowledge reserves, who's basically the outside world's cognition lives by imagination, only then do they slowly become unbelieve and begin to rationalize when life experience increases." Tian Lei also thought that "children may lose much happiness unique to their innocent age if they are taught acting."

Li Yike added that "an actor's ability to control their emotions is important; bringing their audience to the world of fantasy by one's emotions is also important." Mi Zeng, an actor, said that "the core of acting is trueness. The actor must totally believe in what he or she is performing and feel the true emotion interlinked with his role or about to play." Tian Lei shared that "reading minds of roles all the time, knowing who human beings are in other dimensions, and learning acting can improve actors' sophistication. Portraying different characters can give pieces of grand new life experience to actors."

Dr. Sean Wang Yang, a director, said:

> An actor achieves a personal transformation or a transpersonal state when they portray a role. An actor has to seek to turn part of his or her personality into the actor's role. According to Russian dramatis, you have to hate the one you want to kill, even want to eradicate them summer. Such a strong feeling can be used as a so-called "seed" to grow your empathy for the role of a character who wants to kill someone. For instance, if you are a man of masculinity while your role is drinking a cup of tea with the pinky up, an actor must broaden oneself towards such an image. No matter how masculine the actor, there will be some appreciation of female charm they have ignored in your mind. What they have to do next is to penetrate the part of their personality into the role.

Yi Na, an actor, said that when she graduated, everything

changed. Acting has gradually refined me through the four years. Acting also contributes to society; Yi Na spoke of the contributions of acting to actors themselves, their relationships with their families and other people, and society. Echoing Yi Na, participant Zhang Xiaoming said that "people benefit from acting. Acting or directing enabled me to have a deeper understanding of the nature of human beings." To rephrase, it could be said that directors and actors are used to and good at analyzing the details of scripts, roles, and relationships, so when they see a tiny detail or a subtle eye contact of someone, they can interpret and easily understand. It also becomes easier (through practice) for directors or actors to see people's nature right through external details. Directors may see more things than others. From Zhang Xiaoming's perspective, people do benefit from acting to some extent.

Now that the reader has become acquainted with the 10 participants (established Chinese performers), the seven themes and 28 subthemes discovered through data analysis are discussed. Starting with theme one, "participants' definition(s) of acting," which contains four subthemes.

Theme 1: Participants' Definition of Acting

According to this study's participants' views, acting does not have a single and straightforward meaning because almost every participant looked at acting from a different perspective. For many, acting performs many objectives: It stimulates excitement, understanding, controversy, perception, or even intuition. It prompts people of their past and neglected times, or it bestows to them a glance of a possible future when actors see alternative personalities and thinking. It characterizes raw, unadulterated, susceptible—and at moments terrible —astonishing humanity. This concept emphasizes the continuity and diversity of acting. If we try to tune in to someone's essence, we will discover a variety of personality traits. This may be the reason that acting does not have a single explanation upon which everyone agrees. As highlighted by some actors, acting is more of a calling that someone has decided to partake and pursue. Li Jiahang replied:

> *The connection between performance and life reminds me of the Stanislavsky system I learned when I was in Shanghai Theatre Academy. This system teaches actors to analyze people's motivations, desires, etc. These things can help you interpret human nature or understand better and deeper about human life. For example, we might not understand other's behaviors or their motivations when we are young, but we can master the whole line of things through acting. I feel that if we analyze characters and roles in this way, we can also better understand life. In addition, it may help people in emotional expression by seeing the world from an artistic perspective. I think that for many people, art may be something when they are lonely, they can listen to the music they like, or that they enjoy this lonely status for it being a spiritual dependence. The conventional perspective of acting examines what the research population considered as the definition of acting. Indeed, it helps peo-*

ple draw on how the individuals perceive acting as a career that extends to their lifestyles. From the various actors that were assessed, it is very clear that acting is something that they have done for quite some time and it has been the definition of their daily lives.

Another statement from participant Ren Chengwei highlighted the definition of acting from his experience of being in the acting industry for more than 3o years. When asked "How long have you been engaging in drama?" He answered:

I have been on the path of drama and acting for more than 3o years, yet my path to drama is not the same as others. Nowadays, students have their clear goals when they enter college. However, at that time, there were very few college students. Going to college is a turning point in life for me. At first, I tried it out and finally succeeded, so I didn't set limits on myself in life so that I can try more possibilities.

From his perspective, acting is harvested from life experiences that have various possibilities and unlimited potential. Some doctrines believe that acting is a natural ability for everyone, and acting occurs in all spheres of life, even outside of the film industry. Lei Guohua, a productive and reputative director, explained his captivating journey of becoming a director. He explained how the reasoning behind the need for diverse creativity and innovation in the industry. Indeed, actors, directors, scriptwriters, and producers are responsible for developing content that will be engaging and informative to the audience. These people create an energy that goes like a river, a stream, or a flow that, for the creator, can feel like fluidity:

> *Why do we say that acting has a fluid nature? The term refers to the fact that a fluid, once placed in a container, takes on the shape of that container. Acting is thus a fluid art. The performers are at their best when they take on the form of the character, they are currently playing. If acting is viewed as primarily interpretive, the actor's outside characteristics are usually emphasized. However, when acting is seen as a craft of ingenuity, it leads inevitably to looking for the more profound qualities that strengthen the actor's creative ability and affectability.*

> *This looks problematic. The actor must master the first delicate fabric accessible to any skilled worker, the living life form of a human being in all its manifestations, mental, physical, and enthusiastic. The simplest example in this regard is that an on-screen character can be the piano and the pianist at the same time. Like a tennis player, a tennis racket is actually the player themselves. They are immersed into the game that they cannot differentiate between their arms and the rackets and this approach allows them to achieve well.*

In order to enhance the quality of content, scripts are pre-written and roles are assigned based on their natural abilities. Consequently, scripting enables the creation of the end product while affecting the actors' experiences in their roles. According to this perspective, the definition of acting also includes actors immersed in their roles (a theme several participants discussed and explained in the following subtheme).

Acting is Like Everyday Action

Some participants believed acting is an everyday action that people engage in both consciously and unconsciously. For instance, I asked Ren Chengwei, "What makes a good show? How to become a director capable of healing psychologically?" To which he replied,

> The ultimate purpose of the performance is psychological. Performance is something that we all experience on a daily basis, whether we realize it or not. It is of great value to your readers that you have researched this subject. The research studies on psychology, the good or bad of the role completion, are highly relevant to the psychological expressions that are correct, accurate, and meaningful. As I said, every human being in the world is acting on a constant basis, sometimes unconsciously, sometimes consciously, and they are usually rich in acting because they understand very well what they want. We look at it from another perspective when we play the role of someone else. In our minds, we visualize the possible behaviors of an individual and the consequences that result from those possible behaviors. Whether in language or in form, everything is ultimately a psychological expression.

As he said, acting is influenced by the observation of people, which includes understanding their behaviors and motivations.

He described that a person may not be clear in his own mind, but the analysis of others is often spot on. Actors can comprehend the points of view of others that may differ substantially from their own. In fact, actors can usually observe the specific details, very directly and very objectively, showing that the person is representative of an individual's psychological behavior. He declared distinctly that the central aspect of acting is control, and the central aspect of performance is modification. For example, if an actor plays a nice person throughout the role, we do not play a myth. We must present the person's growth and change, including psychological changes. He elaborated by saying, "Yes, life is a trick; we are undergoing a process of change; life is change." Accordingly, with these efforts, a good performance will come from capturing the changing processes of people's daily lives.

It is important to note that actors do not pretend to be another person when depicting human behavior. Rather, they use several strategies to embody the person they would like to be, to feel and act as if they were that person. They cannot become that person if all they do is understand them in their mind. However, they become the character by using their entire body. I asked Li Jiahang, "What is your opinion on the impact of performance on life?" to which he replied:

The connection between performance and life reminds me of Stanislavski, the system I studied during my time at Shanghai Theatre Academy. The system teaches actors how to analyze people's motivations, desires, and so on. These theories and practices can help you interpret them or gain a deeper understanding of life. For example, we may not comprehend others' behavior when we are young; however, we can master the whole line of things by acting. I believe this kind of context can also provide greater insight into life. Furthermore, it may help me express myself emotionally by seeing the world through a different perspective.

From his experiences, he develops his acting skills based on his attempt to bring perspective to his daily life.

Additionally, he informed that all courage of life, including understanding and acting, must be understood. Indeed, as actors, the more comprehensive our dimension, the more deeply we understand the role, the better we comprehend its core. While constructing characters, we create a preliminary setting, which is the aspect of the brain that can be achieved through reading and interpretation. The actor needs to explore this role in greater detail. At this level of analysis, we can more fully believe that this person exists, and we can rely more on the essence of this individual. By this we mean that we want to find a way to consider the significance of these phenomena, especially in the work of actors. I believe that all directors should be profoundly knowledgeable about the role and the play's rhythm, regardless of if they direct film or television. As a result, acting is established from the repeating exploration of our inner worlds—as explored in the next subtheme.

Acting is a Complex of Life Experiences and Situational Thinking

Participants believed that either acting is a complicated or an easy process. Some participants considered acting complicated because it discusses people's complicated lives, and some people considered it easy because, in their school of thought, acting is simply an instinct. The psychological nature of acting makes it complicated, as it deals with the depiction of real-life situations. The role assigned to the actor should be performed effectively; in some cases the role goes beyond the script. Ren Chengwei said,

> *I think it is very easy for actors to reach this state. Because when we play a role, we cannot escape from ourselves and enter into the role, it is easy to transcend ourselves, so I mainly do psychological work in this area. Performing is an effortless thing. It is as simple as you say the word and move the schedule from point A to point B. Nevertheless, this is also a very complicated topic because you have to show a character and character's mind, family status, professional status in a short period. The more information they express, the better their performance is. Performance is a kind of interpretive behavior.*

Mi Zeng shared his view that acting is a complicated process stating,

> *Because acting is about people's natural instincts. My teacher had ever told me when I was on stage, he cried. At that time, all those who had scolded him apologized to him for being wrong about him. He cried more and more heavily. He couldn't stop... Well, teachers can only tell them methods or techniques and give them a guide while a good actor cannot be grown without his or her self-cultivation. Everyone has some gift for performance, more or less. There is a saying that children are the best actors. Why? Because children are themselves. They have no acting techniques, and they keep no lens awareness. They are innocent in his reaction. They behave naturally as animals or people in documentaries, which react all by the primitive instinct without any considerations or scruples. An ideal performance must be as innocent as children.*

According to participants, the definition of acting can vary depending on the context of the play's themes and message, which also determines its complexity. In some events, extensive training is necessary to bring the best out of the actor's talent. The goals behind creating the content and its nature influence the actors' capacities to play their roles and the overall experience.

Acting is Having the Right Technique

When questioned "what is acting," a participant's response

often implied their acting techniques. Participants responded this way because acting techniques are a defining process of becoming an actor; there is no actor if there is no acting technique. In this way, a definition of acting and an acting technique are intertwined. However, participants' response on acting techniques varied in terms of how it defines acting. One group of participants believed acting has no universal technique — that by gaining experience, one can perform acting flawlessly; while others believed that acting has three components. When asked, Lin Hongtong said,

> *They have no acting techniques, and they keep no lens awareness. They are innocent in their reaction. For an actor, with the accumulation of his life experiences and performing skills, the instinctive reaction is more and more difficult to keep. That is why the more experienced an actor is, the more difficult for him to keep real in acting.*

Meanwhile, other participants believed that acting has three components: concealment, inclusiveness, and complexity. This implicates that acting is a broad field that primarily involves dramatizing specific attributes in society. Therefore, actors are tasked with ensuring that their roles help pass the message's theme efficiently.

Acting Has No Specific Definition

As previously stated, some participants believed acting has no specific definition, highlighting that it depends on where it is being applied. Some participants expressed that the application of acting defines its meaning as it can take different approaches. The central point is basing acting on a presentation of specific ideas, cultures, and ideologies. Accordingly, Mi Zeng said,

Acting is something not only about actors on the stage but also about people in daily life. When we are talking about acting, we are talking about human beings and the essence of them, for among different situations, actors switch through different feelings, emotion, actions and so on…It is difficult to use a kind of technique to define acting. Acting differs from a mathematical or a physical question, which demands a single standard answer. "One thousand readers, there are one thousand Hamlets." So do actors. There is no such technique that can enable you to cry as soon as possible in acting as long as you carry out a specific process. Acting doesn't have any best answer. Performance is acceptable as long as it is according to the logic of life.

Zhang Xiaoming said:

Never complicate the meaning of acting and never form acting scientifically, which is what I want to say. That's why children, with a wild imagination, are natural actors. They think creatively. They love making up stories. And in their stories, they naturally have roles. As we know, acting is something about the stage, but actually, acting is a part of life. Every day people are acting from all walks of life.

To put Zhang Xiaoming's claims in another way, it can be said that there is fictional and real-life dramatization. For the fictional segment, the content is a product of imagination not applicable in real life. However, the underlying theme and message are based on aspects that go hand in hand with realities in life, such as people's desire to explore the universe beyond earth. The possibility of having another form of life beyond the planet is backed by justifiable scientific evidence. This, in turn, broadens the scope covered by professional acting and increases its complexity. The fluidity of acting ensures that there is a general flow of the acts such that they have a base that they are based on. Now we move on to theme two, "acting transcends mere skills," and its six related subthemes.

Theme 2: Acting Transcends Mere Skills

To achieve the heights of glory, an actor must develop credibility. An actor should have the ability to enable the audience to believe in him. The ability to convince is considered a key factor for characters to appear credible. As far as skills are concerned, an actor is more than just an imitator. External and internal gestures of an actor describe the symbolic significance of the character being performed. Neither is acting simple exhibitionism, that is, the capacity for "showing off" or engaging at parties is very diverse from the ability requested of the actor—the capacity to put oneself into another character, to form through execution a nonexistent occasion and bring it to its consistent fulfillment, and to rehash this execution, not as it were when one is in a positive disposition, but too at indicated times and places, notwithstanding if one possess sentiments on each event. Certain factors directly impact acting in profound ways, which is a phenomenon of interest in this study.

The questions posed during participant conversations helped determine what the practitioners consider to be the key influencers of acting beyond skills. These factors have an impact on how the actors play their respective roles. They should be considered in arriving at a holistic approach to handling the depiction of key themes and messages. Participants highlighted six major factors essential in acting: (a) deep feeling for life events, (b) conveying emotions effectively, (c) the life experience of actors, (d) going beyond basic performance training, (e) being a well-read individual, and (f) the ability to make emotional connections. The following sections explain each of these factors.

Deep Feeling for Life Events

This factor exists because some elements of acting need to create a more realistic environment of what the scripted phenomenon entails. Some participants believed the performer's life experience must be interlinked with their role to produce an excellent performance. For example, an ability to feel love, frustration, happiness, and passion is crucial to acting. By large, actors should blend the script content and its relation to real-life, extending to their personalities.

Lin Hongton said,

With a great accumulation of performing techniques and life experiences, an experienced actor is not easy to keep 'innocent,' for he has confronted with so many things that they are not fresh or touching anymore for me as before, so every time before I perform, I would return myself to zero. I try to empty my mind, discarding all my performing skills, life experience, and stereotypes. I regard myself as a blank sheet of paper, which would be pictured by me, directors, scripts, lens, and my equals.

Conversely, Mi Zeng said,

A good performance is inseparable from the profound life experiences of actors. Several days ago, one of my colleagues got divorced from her husband. We sat together and had a chat. She said something thought-provoking: Divorce is full of pain, but the experience of getting divorced is a treasure for an actor.

In short, participants believed that the performer's life experience must be interlinked with their role to produce an excellent performance. The experience and ability to feel a range of emotions is crucial to good acting. By relating the script content to real-life emotions an actor can portray deep feelings.

Conveying Emotions Effectively

Actors must possess complete control over their emotions; they must show sadness (shed tears) and joy (smile) when their role requires it. Li Yike assessed his review on controlling emotions by explaining,

> Let me first say that personally, the skill I most desire in performance is to control emotions freely. I don't know what kind of method can ignite my tears instantly, but I asked all these teachers who teach acting, and the answers I got are basically no such method. The difference between a master and an average actor is the different ways to accomplish this. In fact, sometimes crying may not be the best expression. There may be better choices than crying. But sometimes, a special cry may poke people's hearts more directly. At that time, I really wanted to have the ability to control emotions freely because not all crying was touching, but there must be a cry that others could not bear when they saw it.

As Li Yike explained, emotional displays are integral in acting, which makes it seem real and more engaging. This makes the content relatable to the theme message and its application in real-life situations.

Life Experience of Actors

The acting (the performance) is always closely related to the actor. The artistic effect of various roles an actor plays not only depends on his acting skills but also on his inner world. Every new role the actor explores gives him new life experience and insight; every breakthrough that the actor means new adventure in his life. What makes acting most exciting lies in the discovery and growing up of life itself. Real acting is the ability to bring the creator and audience into the performance by making excellent soul communication with the role, other actors, and the audience. Indeed, a high-level actor knows something about the science of life and human beings and knows how to tap into that knowledge.

One of the participants highlighted that the actor's lifestyle also plays an important part in how well they perform in a role. Their lifestyles determine their experiences, which in turn has an impact on role-playing due to the array of experiences they can draw from. However, actors can handle niches that stretch beyond what they have experienced personally through practical training and practice. Therefore, the acting process serves as a platform for gaining new knowledge to expand what is already at hand.

Li Jiahang shared his view stating,

I think what shaped the actors may not be the born of external conditions, but a lifestyle. For example, Johnny Depp and Fan Wei have their respective lifestyles. Different lifestyles create different understandings of the world, which is different artistic aesthetics, including choice of things, so you will see two different people.

In other words, the accumulation of performing experience should not rely on others' preconceived concepts and examples but more on the observation for life. Since performing is an art for, of, and by human beings, it is inseparable from humans' daily lives, so the most important thing for actors to do is go deep into diverse people and their daily lives. This will enable the actors to bring out the real picture and create the environment that suits the script and meet the expectations of the target audience. However, the most important thing in acting is the control of the emotions. An actor must be able to take control their emotions in order to portray the real character.

Beyond Basic Performance Training

Going by significant statements, the participants revealed that basic experience as an actor is an essential element of acting that cannot be overlooked. Despite claims that acting is a natural skill, there is a dire need to offer professional actor training. The training process is used to impart fundamental acting skills that are used by others in the field. It also helps actors realize their weaknesses and strengths to come up with improvement strategies.

Li Jiahang shared his view saying:

> *The single actor performs better because it is his true condition. That said, today, I would feel that the acting can be completed, but the most classic must be more compatible. The excellent actor can accomplish anything, but his most observed role must be what he wants to say to the world, which is the sum of his life.*

I questioned Tian Lei, "Has the audience ever noticed such an interesting interlude?" The audience ought to have taken a very keen observation on an actor's dominant behavior that can uniquely identify him or her. He replied: "Yeah, sometimes they can feel it. But not only does it not spoil the performance, it makes the performance indescribably better."

Being a Well-Read Individual

One of the participants, Ren Chengwei, highlighted that actors need to have a high literacy level, such as reading fiction and non-fiction. An intelligent person will easily master these and have high literacy levels as they easily comprehend things. The essence here is to increase one's general knowledge, which is critically helpful to actors in effective communication and team playing in the cast. Educational institutions offer training through theater and film courses, but acting courses do not often have a high focus on literary competence. Most Chinese actors lack basic literacy knowledge; they do not like reading.

In our conversation, I expressed to Ren Chengwei about Chinese actors lacking in reading by asking "What is the best way to make up for the shortcomings caused by little reading?" He gave this resolution:

> *Observing life, experiencing life, listening to others and thinking more, this is the only way to make up for the emptiness of the brain, and only partially. I like reading and observing life, so I can often observe parts that others do not notice.*

Mi Zeng gave a story about how general knowledge helped an actor:

> *People who have knowledge doesn't always have cul-*

tural awareness. I know a National Class-A Actor who even never went to high school. He always has a profound understanding of roles. Once, he went to an audition that many actors were interested in. Every actor had an opportunity of only 20 minutes. But eventually, he had 1 hour. Why? Because he showed more understanding even than the director. The director appreciated him very much and eventually gave the popular role to him. What enables him to understand the role well is his observation of daily life. He is always curious about everything.

The Ability to Make Emotional Connections

Finally, most participants believe that having an emotional connection with any given_role (empathizing with the role) is the critical factor in being a good actor. It gives the actor the right edge for handling emotions.

First, Li Jiahang shared his thoughts, "Bring emotions in the acting process into life is an absolute energy consumption, which is a torture for life." Next, Lin Hongton put forward his views:

> *I believe that a role, for an actor, is a perfect outlet for their diverse emotions. Sometimes, the roles the audience sees on the screen are far from their actors. When I perform, I always try to find something I also possess from the role I play. Even it is a tiny or minor trait, I can squeeze into the seemingly inaccessible role through the little gap or crack, have empathy with it, and then entirely become it.*

> *When I have become the role, through it, I can discharge*
> *my own personal emotions and feelings which is inter-*
> *linked with that   of the role ... Some actors don't get a lot*
> *of emotions if they have not experienced many exercises.*
> *Practice makes perfect, skillful, and refined, and strives for*
> *perfection.*

In other words, the primary teaching of acting is to let im-
merse the student in an emotional state in advance to make the
person a more effective performer. Observing life, experiencing life, listening to others, and thinking more is the only way
to make up for the brain's emptiness, and only partially. They
are usually stored in the emotion bank through observation
and accumulation. For example, I asked Mi Zheng, "When you
are crying on the stage, do you find the feeling of acting?" He
said yes. He felt the true emotion interlinked with the role he
played. He will always remember the feeling.

In the next theme I explore participants' views on what
can limit an actor's ability to perform. This theme includes five
subthemes.

Theme 3: Things that Limit an Actor's Ability to Perform

There are various challenges experienced by actors in the
field which limit their performance. Achieving a complete
transformation to the desired character is a challenge. This is
due to factors like personalities and stage phobia. Actors are

required to be emotionally present to showcase the character's psychological state which should be relatable to real life experiences.   Moreover, there is a high number of roles which require actors to make transpersonal variations. Sometimes, playing a role might involve going against the individual's beliefs thereby posing a challenge. Participants revealed that it is difficult for actors to put out a good performance without having real-life experiences that can be interlinked with the role. As such, individuals cannot perform all types of roles; it is therefore important for actors to understand their strengths and weaknesses.

Character transformation is deeply psychological, taking up a role with no emotional connection would result in a bad performance. On the other hand, motivation from the audience serves as emotional support. Consequently, how the audience reacts determines if it will be a motivating or discouraging factor for the role-player. It is advisable for actors to focus on their strengths in order to increase the level of engagement with the audience. Actors are required to do thorough training and cast trials before the final product or performance events. According to the respondents, basic training and personal experiences help the actor transform psychologically.

Failure to Perform

From participants' expert opinions, one limit to the profession of acting is the actor's ability to perform. Though actors are very capable of performing various roles, there are still some things that become specific. For example, the negative role is not purely justified by all the actors, but those who do justice with it must have the ability to perform, otherwise it would not be possible for single human being to know the psychology, emotion, and mindset of a lot of people. That is why it is a very important characteristic and quality to distinguish between the really talented people and those who are not capable are just mocking the dialogues and wasting their and audience time in this way. As Ran Changwei said: "Know yourself. My bottom line is that I can't perform an 18-year-old person even if offered huge financial reward. Fresh students without basic performance training shouldn't go out to shoot, which will devastate and disgust themselves."

Lack of Real Experience

In the inquiries of many participants, it was said that if they are not able to experience the condition and scenario, they would never be able to give their true emotions on the stage. The real experience is the thing that will discriminate many of the acting skills. Because it is obvious that the person who has not experienced the real show can't even justify the character. The person who has gone through all the bad and good circumstances can value emotion more than anyone. Thus, it is very necessary for actors to have many experiences. As Lei Guohua said:

If there is no real experience in your life, you will not understand what the performance is, you will not understand the depth of the work. Let me tell you, the drama is from a life whose charm came from life. In fact, as what you just said, the drama and the transformation of characters are highly relevant to the psychological experience what we can touch people is what we have faced in our life.

An Inability to Switch Roles Seamlessly

Participants highlighted that playing a role differently is the greatest challenge to any actor, highlighting that switching how the viewers perceive the same role involves much mental mapping. Roles are formed on specific character traits and circumstances which reflect something in real life or fiction. The actors are expected to act in line with the character roles described. Over the years of acting, a performer masters how to play different roles while remaining captivating and pleasing. Practice over time enhances expertise through interaction, training, and personal improvement thereby reducing weaknesses.

Ren Chengwei said,

> *The greatest difficulty is when the same type of role is played differently, whether it is a stage play or a movie. I think that performing different roles is not a breakthrough, but performing the same role to show different aspects, is the biggest breakthrough.*

Lin Hongton also passed his view regarding different roles:

> *When I received a different role, I didn't actually create it at this stage. Before a few days, other characters and ordinary life were accumulating, and they were all precipitated.*

The actor can produce an 'oneness' state beyond the performance in combination with the camera, the opponent, and the self.

Additionally, Tian Lei shared his view on the subject:

It seems difficult for actors to create different roles. But in fact, an outgoing person may feel embarrassed under some circumstances. A nice guy would have the dark side of the character. Everyone has something deeply hidden in mind that even they themselves have never noticed.

Flexibility in acting increases the number of roles that can be handled by the actor. This makes it an essential ingredient for acting strengths and abilities. Courage and drawbacks determine who is good at acting and those who is not. Logically, not everybody can dramatize an absolute scenario excellently. Actors are frequently under pressure to adapt to new roles within their careers. They handle the pressure by considering these factors essential in acting.

Limitations of Teachers

Participants revealed teachers' limitations, highlighting that teachers cannot teach extreme relaxation and extreme attention; actors need to learn certain techniques themselves. There is a dire need to ensure that actors get the necessary basic training. The respondents indicated that those joining the industry require proper guidance on the appropriate steps to develop their skills. The knowledge acquired should be put into practice while actors gain more from casts, dramas, and play. Lin Hongtong has shared plenty of reviews in this case. He said,

> *Too many teachers think of acting as a skill, a standardized education, and train three different students into exactly same. How do you think about it? The three actors are different. Therefore, I said that the performance cannot be exactly same. The teacher must tailor each unique individual, taking advantage of one's life experience, the characteristics of life, as well as his strengths and weaknesses . . . I noticed that nowadays, some teachers arrange a drama for kids, but there are leading roles and supporting roles, but children cannot choose roles they like from the bottom of heart, which is harmful to their development and confidence. They need to let children understand what the core of acting is, rather than satisfying the vanity of parents . . . I think the responsibility of the teacher, in fact, is to find the right role for your child. The acting profession is more suitable for transpersonal psychology. The reason is that we are constantly seeking our own roles in the process of self-transcendence.*

Mi Zeng passed his views regarding the responsibilities of a teacher by stating,

> *A performing teacher is like a miner, digging out rare jewels and precious stones from his actors by trying as much as possible to help them "feeling" or "touching" their*

roles. Those jewels and precious stones are the gifts for act-ing.

Difficulty in Dramatizing the Details

The study participants indicated that dramatizing individual character details when acting is a complicated process; this is mainly because other parts of the character's life (family, professional life, etc.) must be included in the act. The final product should be an exemplary display of the character in the role. This is affected by many issues such as environment and individual differences from the role played. Success in acting involves playing different roles effectively. Thus, the actor must harness versatile role-playing capabilities. They should be able to dramatize every detail attributed to the role they are playing. The audience is engaged and captivated when they can relate to the ideas being shared and consider them genuine. Lin Hongton said:

> *Just because I am an actor, I will not ignore tiny details in daily life; just because I am an actor, I was responsible for capturing some unimpressive but wonderful moments. If I was not, I would let them brushing [sic] past my hands unconsciously. So as long as an actor stay[s] true to his original self, he can maintain himself.*

Mi Zeng also shared his view: "With the experiences of acting, you tend to notice and feel those details. In the way, you are able to enhance the understanding for human beings."

Tian Lei said, "To achieve that, you have to collect all details of the role, with the help of those phenomena piece together a whole story of him and empathize with the role. It is quite difficult." For specific details of the dramatization to be captured, the actor needs to have placed themselves in that situation or at least have experienced them so that they may be able to bring out the right information, that includes the emotions, tone, and mood of the acts.

In the fourth (of seven) themes, which is shared next, five subthemes emerged, each pertinent to this study's focus.

Theme 4: Integration of Roles

Role integration is a transpersonal process defined as the actor's ability to absorb or enter a role. The integration of roles means that the actor should empathize with the character they are playing. An actor's job is empathy. Its result is the imitation of a character with specific attributes denoted by the series of events. Thereby, role integration is a core element in acting. The phenomenological analysis reveals that the following five factors affect role integration.

Control Over Emotions

Having comprehensive control over emotions is an attribute that aids role integration. Li Yike shared his reviews in such a way,

> *Let me first say that personally, the skill I most desire*

in performance is to control emotions freely. don't know what kind of method can ignite my tears instantly, but I asked all these teachers who teach acting, and the answers I got are basically no such method. The difference between a master and an average actor is the different ways to accomplish this. In fact, sometimes crying may not be the best expression. There may be better choices than crying. But sometimes, a special cry may poke people's hearts more directly. At that time, I really wanted to have the ability to control emotions freely, because not all crying was.

I also talked with Mrs. Lu who expressed,

According to the actor's experience, each person is like a bank that stores emotions. In many cases, there are not so many improvisations. In fact, they are usually stored in the emotion bank through observation and accumulation. When needed, they are extracted instantly then interpreted.

Cultural Awareness

Cultural awareness or prior knowledge of culture aids in role integration. Participant Wang Yang said it best when discussing children and acting:

Let's imagine it: if a foreigner is provided with a menu introducing all kinds of dishes from Chinese eight main culinary schools, he will be confused. Obviously, he has never been familiar with Chinese dishes and cultural traditions before, so he has no idea about how to choose dif-

ferent dishes according to seasons, food materials or the weather. Thus, he has to randomly order something, and it turns out that he doesn't like it. He has another try and fails again. Then he has a bad impression on Chinese food and won't be interested in anything about Chinese food. However, if from the beginning there is a native Chinese who patiently introduces some Chinese dishes suitable to his taste, gradually he himself will find his favorite Chinese dishes. Similarly, since acting has the characteristic of complexity and offers too many choices to children, they need scientific guidance from the beginning; or else, they tend to get lost or even lose all interests about acting and even other artistic forms.

Creation of Environment and Characterization of Roles

Role integration requires the creation of an environment and the characterization of roles to fit what is being displayed. Li Yike said:

After learning to perform, it is easier to capture effective information and focus on the key points. The essence of learning is to create an understanding of how to bring into life what is being acted such that it reflects on the real ideas behind the scripts. Regarding the situation and the relationship of the situation, you can understand the most accurate situation and the relationship of the people, which determines the attitude of how to communicate with it. It is also possible that your goals in life will be clearer.

Tian Lei shared his views:

'To complete a role' and 'to create a role' are two totally different things. If you want to 'create a role' or to bring the character to life, you should be focused and determined and pay all your attention to the role, without being distracted by the outside world, especially yourpartner. If you always pay attention to and wait for your partner's predesigned reaction yet one day your partner gives a wrong reaction, you will feel embarrassed and overwhelmed. However, if you focus on yourself and live your life on the stage without any distraction, you will naturally react to any change, for at that time you are living, not acting anymore.

Life Experiences

The more life experiences a person has, the higher the rate of being able to connect with the role. Li Yike shared his thoughts:

I think that the richness of the character is changing with the increase of life experience when shaping a character, because all the things you can shape are your understanding of life. I use the reserve of life for acting, and when you really have action, you have a sense of faith. Of course, I have also heard that some actors can't get out of the character after they finish roles.

Honing

Honing means exercise. Participants highlighted that exercise improves their focus and alertness level and increases their tolerance level. I asked Lin Hongtong: "What do you think is honing? What kind of honing is important for actors?" He replied:

> *Honing is … exercise. Exercise is the best teacher, making you brave and more powerful. Actors don't get a lot of emotions if they haven't experienced a lot of exercise. Practice makes perfect, skillful and refined, and strives for perfection.*

Going further, Lin Hongton explained,

> *Honing makes me more focused and takes life seriously. Regardless of the size of the character, the protagonist or the supporting role, the big man or the little person is treated with a sincere heart. Each small character will bring different accumulations that are very essential for the delivery of good performances that go hand in hand to generate an accomplished acting that even the audience will sincerely appreciate, take it seriously, and enrich it to a certain extent will bring about a breakthrough. Pay more attention to life, extract materials from life, and absorb nutrients. More to love life, to understand the diversity of the fate of the world's characters, to be more tolerant and much calmer.*

Other study participants gave an opinion on their experiences in enhancing role integration. For example, I asked Li

Yike, "In addition to enhancing self-confidence, how do you think acting can help you?" He said:

The first is to make money economically. The second is to know myself better psychologically, I will consciously analyze myself and introspection. For example, I start to consciously discover the shortcomings of my personality, and then start to discover the strengths and weaknesses of in my own human nature, which are insurmountable, which need to be maintained forever, and which are given by my parents. I began to find the shadow of my parents, and then judge that I am better than them, or not as good as them.

There are claims that role integration has a transpersonal edge and heavily influences the end product from acting. The role plays a specific function in the play, which calls for appropriate integration between the traits and the actor's capabilities. Trainers and those responsible for assigning roles should be keen on ensuring an appropriate application and reflection of various character roles. The responses indicated that a transpersonal approach to role integration comes in handy in getting the best role illustration. A compelling blend between personal attributes and role definitions is required for the process. The participants of the study had the following three things (the three subthemes of theme five) to say regarding their experiences in role integration.

Theme 5: What Leads to a Good Performance

We see a lot of actors on different media platforms, but when we observe closely, we find that only few of them are considered great actors by the audience and the general public. The key characteristic is powerlessness or vulnerability. The on-stage characters must act out the components included within the analysis in arrange to get any concrete advantage from it; something else and it may stay shallow or only mental. Incredible on-stage characters put aside their possess identities, and discover humanity in indeed the darkest of characters. It is this depiction of human feeling that is key to performing in a way that permits groups of onlookers to get it the complex dialect. Exemplifying Shakespeare's plays here.

While investigating the reason for this, an observer concludes that the repetitive good performances of the actor are what made him achieve the place which so many others dream for everyday and every night. Properties of a good performance include:

- Connection between the actor and the role
- The coordination between actor and director
- The relationship between act and the audience

Analyzing the Role and Actor Connection

Li Jiahang mentioned,

> *The excellent performance is placed in the fitting space*

and presents an accurate thing, but the director is the one who gives you space. It may be more important for the director to analyze the role, however, the role of an actor in the entire industrial chain cannot be said to be unimportant. Directors have to know when to give what kind of lens, or when to give what kind of light, and where the actor goes can bring out best.

Actor and Director Coordination

Li Jiahang is an expert in theatrical and drama industry. He believes that for an outstanding performance by the actor, he must be able to have a suitable space where he can connect with the role and absorb the character into his personality. For this to be achieved, there must be a well-established connection and coordination between the actors and the director. This is completely dependent on the director of the show as he'll be the one responsible for providing the guidelines to teach and every actor. Director must also have sound technological knowledge so he can make good decisions about use of equipment to enhance the performance given by the actors.

The Actor and Audience Relationship

One participant, Professor Mi Zeng, made a remark that particularly impressed me. He believes that in all the great performances there is one thing which is very common and can help to give a better performance. According to him, this thing is being true to one's path. As an actor, one is supposed to identify himself or herself with the target audience. If an actor believes in what he is performing and feels it, only then he can become a good actor. The quality of an actor is directly linked with the degree to which he connects emotionally with his audience. Mi Zeng said,

All the good performances have something in common. That is the core of acting: the trueness. Without the core, an acting loses everything. The actor must totally believe in what he or she is performing. An actor must feel the true emotion interlinked with the role he is playing or about to play. That's the starting point of a good actor. On one hand, acting is something complicated, for it is about people's life, about human beings. On the other hand, acting could also be something easy to comprehend because acting is about people's natural instincts. A good performance is inseparable from profound life experiences of actors.

Regarding truthfulness Mi Zheng explained:

The thing is being true to one's path. If an actor believes in what he is performing and feels it, only then he can become a good actor. The quality of an actor is directly linked with the degree to which he connects emotionally with his audience.

We now move on to the sixth theme, which contains just one subtheme.

Theme 6: Acting is Rooted in Our Social Status

All human beings are actors. We all react to a particular situation based on our understanding of it whenever we are confronted with one. As I mentioned previously, people are performing all the time, sometimes unconsciously, sometimes consciously, and they are usually good at it, because they know very well what they want. If we can connect to the situation on a personal level, then we will undoubtedly respond to it better than a person who is unable to grasp the situation and remains clueless for the rest of his life. Based on the niche level, new radical social and technological ideas emerge. The actors' work can become a vehicle for social change. By their exceptional ability to communicate, stage characters are communicators. Through their work, they can influence society and shape things to come. Art, including theatre, film, or music, enables individuals from diverse societies to share their stories and experience through images, sounds, and images.

We can also observe that we may not like a lot of people around us. This may lead to conflict and can also lead to a bad reputation if it is displayed in public. However, at the same time, if we can act and control our emotions, we can rescue our society from a possible conflict and we can enable our society to take a big step forward in development, improvement and evolution. From this perspective, people acquire knowledge and practice of acting from dealing with their social status, and they shape themselves as actors from it.

Acting and Social Development

One question I asked participants is whether acting can promote the development of society. Ren Chengwai said: "Of course! Drama has a very good role in promotion because it actually relieves many psychological stresses."

In our modern and developed societies, we all go to work early in the morning and return at night. Consequently, we become tired and frustrated at the end of the day. Acting is a great stress reliever at this point, it is also a great source of entertainment to distract us from our hectic routines.

Good acting leads to a peaceful society which is free from all kinds of conflicts. It allows people to differentiate between good and bad and help them develop a sense of judgment. This will enable a person to stay away from bad things and stay close to the positive things, which will allow the entire society to live and thrive in a better way. When questioned about whether acting contributes to society, Yi Na said:

> Yeah, I sort of agree. Firstly, when you watch a comedy, you laugh; when you watch a weepy film, you shed tears, which is a form of light relief for the audience. Secondly, when you watch the performance, you are from a god-like perspective more or less and you clearly know the relations and conflicts among roles and the reasons behind them, so you can draw some inspiration from them on how to handle problems in a more appropriate way and how to lead a happier life. Acting contributes to the harmonious development of societies to a certain extent. For example, if

there was a conflict between two roles, the audience would be able to recognize the individuals responsible and how it was triggered. Therefore, you will know how to avoid conflict in your everyday life.

From these participants' statements, it is clear that the cognition, values, and attitudes that we put into action are determined by how we have been handled by the society. Finally, the seventh and final theme is explored along with its four subthemes.

Theme 7: The Influence of a Role on the Actor

Studies have shown that acting and performance have a profound effect on human life. They are the tools we utilize to develop our most desired abilities: for example, to analyze a character's emotions and mental aptitude. By acting, we can improve these abilities. Furthermore, it is very important to build moral ethics. A lot of good qualities are associated with the characters and roles that are portrayed in movies and television programs. They will not only enchant viewers, but also inspire the actors to enhance their inner ethics and become better versions of themselves. Acting is an excellent way to relieve stress. Merging into a new human being, a different role from one's authentic self, enables one to acquire a deeper understanding of the psychology of people around them. As human beings, we occasionally struggle with controlling or grasping our emotions. Acting gives us a good opportunity for this. According to this perspective, acting can assist actors in developing their personalities and transforming themselves into better people.

Another important view was brought up by Lin Hongton,

Occasionally, you shed your own mask, which is something everyone in society has, in order to put on a stranger's mask, who is similar but not quite the same as yours. You get some freedom from this process. You get a piece of a brand-new life experience.

An interpretation of this participants' words could be that most people wear a mask to hide their identity, even hiding it to those very close to them. This mask hides their emotions, feelings, tears, and weaknesses while presenting a strong person in the society. Frequently, these masks are altered to face different individuals. In this way, a person can develop multiple personalities and lose focus on the original one. Thus, acting and playing specific roles help actors find their essence and embrace their true natures.

Analyzing People

The participants considered acting as an examination and inspection of behavior. They study different roles that enable them to develop a depth of understanding in different situations. It might help to enhance their emotional expression by allowing them to see experience from an artistic viewpoint. It helps the students learn how to switch between various roles and the importance of valuing attitudes and relationships accordingly. As Li Jiahang said:

> *The connection between performance and life reminds me of the Stanislavsky system I learned during Shanghai Theatre Academy. This system teaches actors to analyze people's motivations, desires, etc. These things can help you interpret them, or they can help you understand better and deeper about life. For example, we may not understand other's behavior when we are young, we can master the whole line of things through acting. I feel that this kind of context can also better understand life. In addition, it may help my emotional expression by seeing the world from an artistic perspective. I think that for many people, art may be that when they are lonely, they can listen to the music they like, or that they enjoy this lonely state, it is a spiritual dependence.*

According to his statement, people will see performing art offers actors new visions to their lives by opening their eyes to others so that they can be mindful to others' life experiences.

Shaping the Character

Through the standpoint of some actors, we have realized that acting has led many people to become new versions of themselves as they relate to the characters they portrayed, which is transformative. Moral values and ethics that heroes embody in their roles influence not only the public but also the actors. As a result, they observed their own positive version.

As it was claimed by Wang Yang,

There are some roles that have changed my life in some ways. For example, my most memorable role was Liu Zhen Xing in a classic TV drama called Annual Ring, in 1992 when I was sixteen years old. It was my first acting experience. At that time, I was quite different from Liu Zhen Xing, who is regarded as a brother of his friends around him, vigorous, exceptionally responsible and caring. While I was playing the part, I did not consider that I was merely a more subdued child, but I was just concentrating on the creation of my character. However, many years later someday I suddenly discovered that his words, his thoughts and his actions had shaped me to some extent. His personality has found its way into my body, and some of his good qualities have manifested in me.

Based on his experiences, people will realize that actors will transform themselves when they act their roles. Actors who play characters in a play internalize the storylines of the roles so as to become their own experiences, which reshapes them in their own lives.

The Therapeutic Effect of Acting

In a world full of hustle and bustle, acting can offer a mental escape and a sense of relaxation. For example, when you are on set, you are fully focused on that task, not even thinking about the problems or confusion you are experiencing in your regular day-to-day activities. In addition, people who possess excellent acting skills and a passion for acting find it enjoyable to portray various roles. It is a way of getting away from our everyday lives. As Mi Zeng said:

> *By acting, some people enjoy mental relaxation, just like what you said before: get   freedom. Acting can be used to gain self-confidence or to improve interpersonal relationships. This is just a part of what playing a part can do for people's lives.*

His experience suggests acting has a therapeutic effect on relaxation and improving social relationships.

The Sophistication Process of Socialization

According to some participants, acting can be a very effective way of developing the emotional well-being needed in life. We can use it to adapt ourselves to the situation and circumstances in which we are currently experiencing. The sophistication of socialization, which is essential in practically all conditions and situations in life, can be greatly enhanced through acting. During acting, people learn how to control their nerves very efficiently. The following quote is from Tian Lei,

> *Acting teaches actors to read minds of characters who are human but in a different dimension, and so can improve their sophistication in society. Furthermore, as we have already spoken about, portraying different characters can give actors a whole new life experience, resulting in*

children being more creative. On the other hand, children
may lose their happiness that is unique to their young age.

From this perspective, acting has a catalyst effect on human development, in that it helps people comprehend their own situations and adapt to society, making them into more mature individuals.

Conclusion

This chapter shared results derived from data analysis of conversation transcripts with 10 participants. Seven themes and 28 subthemes were discussed in detail, using participants' authentic responses as evidence. The following chapter is a thorough discussion of the results shared in this chapter, the main goal of which is to view acting through a transpersonal psychology framework to comprehend the essence of acting.

Chapter 5: Discussion

The thematic results of the phenomenological process with research participants have branched out into many issues of consciousness such as transcendence, spirit, and Self. Many issues and aspects crossover from the seven identified themes. Through the analysis of data combined with the study and research of transpersonal psychology, it is true that transpersonal psychology studies the law of the occurrence and development of human psychological activities, and explores the nature of human psychology to achieve healthy development in social life.

To promote the improvement of the efficiency of various activities in social practice, transpersonal psychology research has its own mystery and complexity; while performance art is lived through the creation of actors—full of flesh and blood, full of distinctive personality, and unique souls—characters with artistic charm also have their own mysteries and complexity. The easiest and the most difficult art in the world is, in the researcher's opinion, performance art. After the combination of two equally mysterious and complex systems, a creative and wonderful process occurs.

In this chapter, the researcher reintegrates the research themes (discussed in chapter 4) into several groups of transpersonal psychology and discuss the transpersonal psychological process of actors according to the system of transpersonal psychology. Specifically, he discusses the following concepts at length: (a) self-transcendence as a perspective of method acting, (b) transcendence via sense memory, (c) transference of spirit, and (d) return to self.

In the literature review (Chapter 2), psychological works that related to the Stanislavsky performance system were referenced. Performing art is a complex, vast, subtle, and sensitive subject. It is precisely because of these characteristics of performance that systematic and feasible methods, skills, and theories are needed. To explore the process of actor's transcending creation of roles and Self, it is essential to incorporate the Stanislavsky performance system as the theoretical basis, using transpersonal psychology's components combined with the thematic phenomena of transpersonal psychology as seen in previous chapters. The conversation's themes are discussed in groups because of participant narrations of situations where transpersonal psychological concepts appear to be at work but are in fact only half-baked. Therefore, the themes do not (and cannot) reach their full potential of what they might be if participants did consciously use transpersonal psychological concepts. Therefore, it needs to be left to the future to discover these potentialities in terms of analyzing and synthesizing a more evolved answer to the question of "What is acting?"

This study brings transpersonal psychology concepts explicitly into the final discussion. In the first theme, the fluid nature of acting, acting is both a complex and an easy process. Results obtained from participants' interviews indicated that most view acting as a complicated endeavor because it addresses peoples' complex lifestyles. Some participants considered acting easy since it's all about instincts. Actors who have self-knowledge and mastered character and identity find acting easy. The use of transpersonal psychology can promote the fluid nature of acting. The most important factor of acting is the second theme. Participants highlighted various factors directly impacting actors while performing, including having a deeper feeling for life events. In this case, transpersonal psychology assists actors with real-life events during acting by providing necessary knowledge to enhance their performance. Therefore, the ability to feel passion, love, frustration, or any other real-life events is vital in acting.

Self-Transformation as a Perspective of Method Acting

This section discusses various concepts of transpersonal psychology. The concept of self-transformation occurs when actors infuse their emotions into their roles in a mindful manner, which reflects themes two and four (discussed in Chapter 4). With these practices, actors will become holistic, enabling them to transform from performing. The research themes revealed from this study's research and discussed herein are applicable to transpersonal psychology concepts because interpersonal psychology addresses human Self-transformation, and this study aims to answer *what is acting*. For an actor to achieve self-transformation, they must be able to draw personal life experience and memories. Life events are the source of performing, they are the data required to train actors effectively. When conflict occurs, when the task is to be solved, actors need to act aggressively in the context of the moment, but they must be clear on two points during the moment: *What am I doing and why am I doing this?* For example, in Shakespeare's drama *Hamlet*, if there is no starting point for the opening event—Hamlet's father killed by the usurper uncle who seized power and the new king marrying his mother—then there will be no act of revenge in which to motivate the character throughout the character's performance. According to this, the starting event was a turning point in the life of the characters; to perform effectively, the actors must be good at understanding how an event plays a role in the lives of the characters, and what actions push him to act out, what led him to thoughts and emotions, and so forth. This is a time in which transpersonal psychology is at play and could be greater harnessed in actor training.

Transpersonal psychology addresses human Self-transformation and in the context of this study, tries to answer *what is acting*. For example, the development of spirituality, consciousness, spiritual evolution, and crisis (see Friedman & Hartelius, 2015). Method acting is the most important methodology and theory in training actors. For actors to achieve self-transformation, actors must draw from personal experience and memories to garner real emotions and connect with characters. In theme two, acting transcends mere skills to also include conveying emotions effectively, actors' life experiences beyond basic performance training, being a well-read individual, and deep feeling of life events. Therefore, self-transformation is key because actors must transcend pure and simple skills. For example, participant Li Yike said that an actor's ability to control emotions is important and transcending this skill is vital; bringing an audience to the world of fantasy by one's controlling emotions is also important, an actor's lifestyle determines their experiences and therefore impacts role-playing. Additionally, participant Li Jiahang said interpreting people or understanding better and deeper about life is attained from having a long-acting experience. He also suggested that acting mostly needs understanding and empathy. The process of transformation as discussed in transpersonal psychology is evident in theme four, *integration of roles*, as actors need to transform to be able to integrate roles when acting. Playing roles differently is considered the greatest challenge in acting. For example, participant Ren Chengwei said that the research studies are psychology, the good or bad of the role completion is highly relevant to the correct psychological expressions, accurate, and rich.

The transformation of actions (by the actor) become the "starting point" of a role's life; transforming physical action became the best stimulation to evoke emotional feelings, and actors will fast forward to complete their "super objective" accurately as long as they follow the action line strictly. In the transforming action method, physical action is not only the purpose and content of the role's reflective process, but it is also the means to achieve goals and the starting line.

Transpersonal psychology can teach actors Self-transformation through acting by enabling integration of an assigned role and a connection with characters/roles through dimensional and different interpretations of self-awareness. This concept helps address the main question *what is acting?* Participant Tian Lei supported this by saying that actors must read the minds of characters all the time, which requires knowing human beings in other dimensions. Because of this, acting can improve an actor's sophistication. Portraying different characters can give pieces of grand new life experience to actors. In other words, participants like Tian Lei suggest that the point of view of self-transformation of transpersonal psychology can enhance actor's method acting training.

There is a complicated process for actors to create roles. One of the premises is that as an actor, the role to be played often has a variety of different personalities and personality characteristics, and these characteristics may not exist in him or even the opposite. Therefore, when playing in the process of the role, the actor will inevitably experience a complex psychological transcendence and a process of psychological adaptation and transformation. From the understanding, experience, and embodiment of the role to the integration with the role, the actor will overcome many of the thoughts of himself and the role. Contradictions in various aspects such as emotions and personality, and at the same time, we must resolve the contradictions between the different backgrounds and living conditions of our own time and the time of the character; transformation is particularly important in the creative process.

There was immense reflection on the research by all participants in the process. The selection and usage of empirical (experiential) and reflective (reduction) methods depended on the
context and nature of the study. It is crucial to understand the
participation of the participants/actors throughout the study.
Phenomenological methods were the source of study and research. First, the researcher collected data about all the actors
through one-on-one conversations. Then, through analysis
and reflection, the researcher reached an understanding of the
phenomenon of acting. Participants expressed that as actors,
they must generate trust and tacit understanding, they complete the creation together, and generate ideological and emotional resonance with the audience, to be affirmed and recognized by the audience. These are the transformation processes
of actors into roles, and many of these ideas are expressed by
Zirilli (2004) as discussed in Chapter 2.

However, according to the analysis of transpersonal psychology principles such as transformation, the phenomenon of
self-transformation and transcendence reflects the subjective
reality of human experience. An actor's performance-creation
process is the actor's craft to create the character's psychology
and the character's inner activities. It is based on psychology
and the law of inner activities and forms its own uniqueness
according to the characteristics and needs of the actor's performance creation.

Transcending the self and transforming the psychological
mechanism of self and the laws of mental activity, participating
in and influencing the performance creation of actors, under-

standing and analyzing the role, experiencing and reflecting the specific perception and reflection in the process of creating the role. Among them, one level is the psychological characteristics and creative characteristics of the actors themselves, and the other is the psychological characteristics and quirks of the characters to be created. These two levels are closely related and inseparable, forming a complex dualistic psychological process. What we want to study here is the psychological transcendence created by actors' performing arts and the laws of psychological transformation.

The above themes are applicable in transpersonal psychology concepts like spirituality, and transformation. For an actor to achieve self-transformation, they must be able to draw personal life experience and memories in a deep and profound way. Interpersonal transpersonal psychology addresses human Self-transformation.

Transcendence via Sense Memory

Themes two and three focus on things that limit an actor's ability to perform. This subsection discusses self-transcendence, a concept of transpersonal psychology in acting. This theme clearly portrays several limitations in acting through the transformation concept of transpersonal psychology. The transformation on an actor to connect to human emotions requires self-transcendence, high mental knowledge, and transdisciplinary thinking.

Transcendence and going beyond self-transformation

impact acting. Transcendence is the existence or experience beyond the physical and normal levels. Sensory memory is a critical technique for acting training that are relevant in our participatory research related to actor training. The ability of actors to experience unique personal self is described as transcend personhood. According to literature, actors who go beyond self-transformation and perform well require intensive and long period of practice. Sensory memory plays a vital role in the performance and going beyond self. Numerous exercises of memory and examination of actors mental, and mental activities promote high level of self-knowledge. In addition, theme 3 on things that limit an actor's ability to perform such as, difficulty in dramatizing the details, limitation of teachers, lack of real experience, inability to switch role seamlessly failure to perform and ability to make emotional connection require self- transcendence, high mental knowledge, and transdisciplinary thinking. Theme four, "factors that aid role integration," discussed that the transcendence of actors requires excellent role and character integration. For actors to self -transcend in roles, high sensory memory is necessary.

The transpersonal psychology concept of transformation teaches actors to go beyond self, such as through mindfulness meditation, to attain a new level of the spirit and consciousness, therefore further perfecting the art of memorizing, switching roles, and many other techniques. Transpersonal psychology helps solve a problem that a person is not oneself in acting through transformation and the transcending actor's ability to perform. Also, through a change of attitude fostered by incorporating transpersonal perspective into the acting practice, we have deeper understanding of how sensory memory works, and with understanding, in turn, sensory memory can help actors achieve day-to-day life activities that constitute acting while off stage.

"Playing the other, showing a different personality" is the main task of actors in creating roles. This requires the actor to be able to create a living, flesh-and-blood character with a personality different from his own. In the creation of roles by actors, actors are not only "creators," but they must also use their own body and mind as "creative materials," and they must use "self-materials" to create "creative products." This becomes a relationship between actors and roles. It must be a relationship of contradiction and unity, and this relationship runs through the entire process of actors creating roles from beginning to end. In my opinion, the entire creation needs to rely on sensory memory to achieve self-transcendence.

In previous performance studies, there was no substantial discussion of sensory memory and self-transcendence in performance. Because in creation, actors and roles have a "dual nature." In the process of an actor "transforming" himself into a role, the life experience, personality characteristics, thoughts, and emotions of the role are unfamiliar to the actor. The actor must accept another set of behaviors and another thought system, which constitutes the contradiction between the actors and the characters.

Regardless of the differences between actors and roles (or characters), actors must recognize, understand, and accept roles through their own sensory memory, and integrate with them, to achieve self-transcendence and create the image of the role with the memory content in the self (Moustakas, 1994). Appearing in front of the audience, the result of this creation is a good solution to the contradiction between the two, forming a unity between actors and roles.

The author of this study suggests that this unification process is the "transformation" of sensory memory. Transformation is not about leaving the self; it is transcending the self. It surrounds oneself with a predetermined situation in the actions of the character, and blends with this situation, so that it is not clear where one person begins and ends and where the character begins and ends. This may be transcendence in the true sense. In my opinion, the actor is both an outsider and a person in the play. Outside the play and in the play, the true and false are the same. Performing art is the art of playing roles and creating character images. Transformed into roles and actors through sensory memory are contradictory and coexistent. They are unified in the creation of character images. In the process of creation, actors use their own sensory memory to interact with characters, transform each other, and jointly promote the process of transcendence.

Actors should be involved in the art of the entire character, together with self-memory, physical form, sound and so on are all in one's being, and the actor's character is to self-transcend in order to effectively and play the role of integration. I think that's what I'm asking of actors in order to become characters. Because of the differences in life experience, personality, thought, and background of the times, there are bound to be contradictions between actors and characters, and actors need to transcend the self in the performance through the memory of life and summon them to become characters, so as to solve this contradiction.

Therefore, actors should do their best to recognize, understand and accept the role, so that they and the role of integration, the formation of unity between actors and characters, at the same time, in the process of creating their own roles, but also do not lose themselves, always communicate with the audience. This is a "double" state, so it must achieve beyond the self to achieve "transition to role" of the "double life." The researcher of this dissertation remembers when he was an actor and shares a brief reflection to further support his argument.

When I was acting, I felt like I was living a double life, crying, or laughing on the one hand, but at the same time parsing my tears and laughter so that they could act most powerfully on the audience he wanted to impress. As an actor, when I lived in the character world, I didn't lose myself. While I was crying and laughing on stage, I was still observing my own laughter and tears; I want to constitute the characteristics of my art, a kind of "double life," that is, a balance relationship between play-as-living and living-as-play. That feeling is wonderful, and its power seems to lift my whole soul. It makes me feel like I can think in many directions. Previously, I could hardly describe the beauty of such a process until I learned to understand transpersonal psychology. I know that this is the transcendence of the self. In short, the performing arts is complex, there are mutual influence and interaction between actors and characters, actors in the performance not only to create a good character image, but also to maintain a sober self, this dialectical method depends on the actor through their own sensory memory of the existence, and constantly explore themselves, to achieve self-transcendence.

The psychological process of the actor's creation of the character includes a complete process of knowing self, to feeling the self, to going beyond the self-over, to becoming the character of understanding and experiencing the character, to embodying the character, meanwhile also includes acceptance and aesthetics of the audience. In this process there are actually two levels, one is their own transcendence.

Transcendental knowledge among actors is promoted by Zehavi (1999) as an extension of both self-knowledge and book knowledge. He describes that intensive practice of numerous exercises of memory, introspection, and body awareness actors tend to give actors a high level of self-knowledge. Actors according to their own understanding of the role, understanding and imagination, as well as life experience and life logic, the use of sensory memory, the way to achieve self-transcendence to create a living character.

The second level is the communication with the audience. Transcendental knowledge and consciousness as interrelated with bodily, linguistic, and spiritual communication is led by Ali (2009), who relates how actors communicate inner experiences to an entire room, sometimes filled with thousands of people. Put forward the display of a character in front of the audience, waiting for the audience's participation, testing and evaluation, that's the second level of actor's psychological process. Actors creating a character itself has psychological complexity, coupled with the need to communicate with the audience, adds the complexity of actor's creative psychology. Communication is essentially about connection and sharing meaning between and speaker and listener, an intimate event. This capacity for uniquely intimate communication in actors can sometimes be thought of as a transpersonal experience that Braud and Anderson (1998) called "maximum personal encounter" (p. 25).

This theme clearly portrays several limitations in acting through the transformation concepts in transpersonal psychology. The transformation on an actor to connect to human emotions require self-transcendence, high mental knowledge, and transdisciplinary thinking.

Transformation of the Spirit

This section explains the transformation of the spirit when acting by examining themes two and four. Both spiritual practice and transformation lead to realization of high human potential; therefore, Self-transcendence in role is vital for each actor self-transformation and going beyond self.

Transformation of actors to better awareness, consciousness, behaviors, experience, beliefs, values, and practices may encourage a personal transformation toward one's higher potential. Transpersonal psychology concepts such as spirituality and consciousness are applicable in theme two "acting transcends mere skills." Actors need to feel life experiences to develop and grow such feelings. For transformations in their awareness to occur, actors have to transcend training skills. Although spiritual heights can be achieved involuntary, every actor must develop self-consciousness throughout. In this case, transpersonal psychology can be used to equip actors to attain a more advanced spiritual practice and higher consciousness through mindfulness meditation, since transpersonal psychology addresses the species' collective interest in spirituality, studies behavior, and experience (Ruzek, 2007).

Spirit or the implicit spirituality, was a vibrant discourse subject during our participatory process. For example, these issues surfaced in the view that acting is a depiction of human behaviors from theme one, "participants' definition of acting." The idea that acting is a complex of life experiences and situational thinking. The psychological nature of acting makes it complicated as it deals with the depiction of real-life situations. As an actor, the role assigned should be performed well and, in some cases, goes beyond the script; deep feelings for life events are crucial for actors, and the importance of lifestyle and experience, for instance.

Li Yike adds that an actor's ability to control their emotions is important. However, bringing one's audience to the world of fantasy by portraying strong emotions is also important. An actor's lifestyle determines their experiences and therefore impacts role–playing and switching roles. In theme three, things that limit an actor's ability to perform spiritually, appears in the guise of meditation and observing life, which also appeared in theme four, where cultural awareness, focus, and meditation are noted as elements of role integration. Lastly, in theme seven "the influence of a role to actor," where mental relaxation, psychological introspection, and understanding life and death are all embodiments of the spirit or spirituality. The remainder of this section presents an interpretation on the connection between spirituality and acting by sharing the work of Benner (2011).

Benner (2011) claimed that Western culture incorrectly conflates spirituality with religion:

> *Many people assume that spirituality is a euphemism for religion. [But] properly understood, spirituality is a dimension of the life of all people . . . It is no more possible for a person to not be a spiritual being than it is to not be an embodied being . . . Everyone has a spirituality, whether they think of themselves as spiritual or not. (p. 23)*

Elaborating, Benner (2011) explained spirituality as "a way of living in relation to that which is beyond the self" (p. 23). According to Benner, a person is directed by their spirituality and a person's spirituality is connected to their transcendent self.

According to Benner (2011) and others, spiritual existence is the basic psychological phenomenon of human beings, and spirit plays an extremely important role in human psychological activities. The spirit of the actor is very far-reaching, that is, via spirit, actors distinguish the character and the role's various attributes. Using color as an example, it can visually bring different spiritual feelings to people. From our experience, when we see green, it brings us a spirit of the natural ecology, calm with vitality, when we see red, and spirit may be excitement and enthusiasm. Paint two equally heavy boxes, one white and the other black, one may feel spiritually that the white box is lighter and the black box is heavier. These are spiritual reactions. Since humanity is by nature a spiritual creature. Personality psychologist Gordon Allport (1937) regarded the "religious sentiment" in its function of "relating the individual meaningfully to the whole of Being" (p. 98) as one of our strongest traits as a species.

These spiritual feelings reflect the various attributes of objective things. Due to different attributes, the spirit of things are divided into many types because it cannot be seen and touched, I would like to call it "external spirit" and "internal spirit," but, whether external or internal spirit, it is an integral experience for us to know ourselves or objective things in the world, and is an important transcendental component of the individual, but also for the actor to achieve the integration of the self and the role in an important way.

The literature of the performance process rarely expresses the concept of self-spiritual transcendence. In the literature, researchers seem to be trying to describe the inevitability of spiritual transcendence, but it is not possible to articulate this concept accurately. The existence of spiritual transcendence is the response to the individual attributes of objective things in the actor's brain, due to the perception of the spirit, to reach our external and internal whole existence, like the gurgling spring water, bright sunshine, dancing light and shadow, melodious sound, the spirit lends the actor in the process of creating the role as a feast. May it be called meditation, or the transcendence of the soul, or we may define it as inspiration. Its existence not only enables the actor to achieve beyond the self at the same time better integrated into the character, but he also affects the actor to better understand themselves.

An actor's inspiration can basically be summed up as an epiphany produced in the unconscious, from a transpersonal point of view (Tart, 1969). The actor's inspiration is processed in the brain's excitement center of the nerve cells in order to seek much-needed character formation and creative materials, after a long period of fruitless but highly conscious and unusually intense exploration and meditation on the role, the actor's own brain's nerve cells suddenly became hyper-active, achieving self-transcendence, mobilize the enthusiasm of the dormant unconscious psychological activity, this unwittingly forms a new way of performing.

Actors will also be triggered by something and suddenly burst out of a spring of thought, an unstoppable motion, and a phenomenon of self-transcendence that is creative. The transcendence in the spirit may stem from the brewing of consciousness and subconscious, which seems sudden, but it is not without seed. In the process of finding a character's own feelings, often many obstacles arise, and it must be the transcendence of the spirit that saves the actor. Therefore, actors should strive to have opportunities for their mind to face and absorb fresh or novel experiences or thoughts, as nourishment of the spirit. It doesn't matter if it's worse than before. The advantage of the spiritual gift is that it is the present, ready to promote the actor's self-creation in the depths of the soul. What's more, in the creative burst of true soul transcendence, who can determine which is good and which is not? They each have their own benefits, all wonderful, because it is the transcendence of our soul! Both spiritual practice and transformation lead to the realization of a high human potential; therefore, Self-transcendence in a role is vital for each actor's self-transformation and going beyond the self.

Return of the Self

Theme two is summarized as acting transcends mere skills. In this theme, one negative aspect of acting discussed by participants is the importance of leaving a role after the performance. Below offers a transpersonal psychological account about returning to self after transformation.

From the various goals of an actor elicited by Stanislavsky, we can think of them as a new single goal, which is to form the regression self of the creative character. In this return-to-self, there is a sense of transcendence of the spiritual material of the character's content and the spiritual material contained in the actor himself. In layman's terms, return-to-self includes the actor's self-return to the "character self" and the transcendence of the "self-self." That is to say, not only the actor creates the character with "duality," the actor's self-return also has "duality"; that is, on one hand, by the actors' own experience and emotion formed by the self-feeling of the character, while on the other hand, it also includes the role itself should be felt from the role due return, that is, subjective sensibility and objective rationality. These two aspects affect each other, and finally reach the fusion, can finally realize the actor's creative role of self-return. Stanislavski (1957/2014) did not make a clear analysis of the return to self, only a vague statement.

However, the return-to-self is self-analysis and evaluation, self-analysis is the understanding, but in our language, understanding means feeling, feeling means returning to the self, and a closure. The analysis required by an actor is quite different from what a scholar or critic needs. If the result of scientific analysis is thought, then the result of actor analysis should be a return to the self. We can say that the post-analysis understanding is the development of self-regression. Actors create characters through analysis, constantly feeling and experiencing, and constantly deepen their understanding of the characters. This requires the actor's solid life accumulation and knowledge and experience accumulation, only through the accumulation, can wake up the real self, return to the true existence of me.

Therefore, the return to the Self is an important factor for actors. Existing life experience is not under our control, and from this point of view, a good actor must carefully choose their own experiences in life, and strengthen learning, accumulated enough knowledge and experience, to form the right sense of creativity, to create a successful play. This factor impacts acting in profound ways. The notion of higher human development is defined somewhat differently in different transpersonal systems, but most characterize it as relating to an expanding and integration of one's sense of connectedness, whether it be with self, community, nature, or the entire cosmos. For a character to appear credible, the actor must convince the audience, and as far as skills are concerned, the actor is deemed more than just an imitator. The capacity to put oneself into another character, to form through execution a nonexistent occasion and bring it to its consistent fulfillment, and to rehash this execution, requires both external and internal gestures of an actor. Transpersonal psychology teaches actors the necessary experience, knowledge, and return to the self through self-awareness and provision of necessary information.

Conclusion

The chapter began earnestly with the analysis of data combined with the study and research of transpersonal psychology. In the early part of the chapter, it is evident that transpersonal psychology studies the law of the occurrence and development of human psychological activities and explores the nature of human psychology to achieve healthy development in social life. Also, this chapter has been able to put forward the vital role of sensory memory as it plays vital role in the performance and going beyond self. Going forward, the transformation of the spirit was also discussed by examining themes two and four. This chapter also provided the relevance of spirituality in transpersonal psychology.

Furthermore, transpersonal psychology concepts are explored explicitly in the final discussion. In the first theme (the fluid nature of acting, acting is both a complex and an easy process), results obtained from participants' interviews indicated that most view acting as a complicated endeavor because it addresses peoples' complex lifestyles. Finally, it transforms themselves in a spiritual way. On the stage, the actor utilizes their sensual memories to expand their consciousness, which forms sensational memories in their body. When their memories are activated, they can quickly ground themselves so that they are able to return to themselves. Therefore, one explanation of acting, which this study seeks to address, is that acting is a process of internal and external transformation. The next and final chapter reflects on the study's key findings and implications and suggests areas of future research.

Chapter 6: Conclusion

Mainstreaming Acting Through
Empiric Transpersonal Psychology

By investigating the behavioral aspects of the human psyche, transpersonal psychology makes a significant contribution to the acting psychology discipline, connecting the transpersonal spirit to a mainstream psychological science. This is
achieved where the basic grounds of transpersonal psychology
and its contribution to mainstream acting psychology lies in
its various perspectives. First, the broadening of transpersonal
psychology concepts such as transformation, spirituality, and
consciousness effecting human potential, Self, and abilities.
Second, its acknowledgment of impulses towards the ideal
states of self-expression, health, and fulfillment. Third, its acknowledgment of the availability of natural, independent, and
alternate facts that can be experienced through a wide range
of consciousness focus. Finally, it recognizes the interdependence of a person's mind and the existence of superior inner
knowledge in experience, dreams, and states of creative inspiration. Transpersonal psychology enhances contemporary psychological perspectives to involve all creations and creatures in
a greater context with higher motives, meaning, and purpose
by drawing attention to the availability of dimensionally greater areas than previously assigned (Metzner, 1989).

Transpersonal psychology helps in understanding various theatrical roles in relation to the progress achieved through the efforts of time. Instead of discussing how an actor gets into a role, we see, from a transpersonal psychology lens, that acting is an easily understood way to achieve self-transformation. That is leaving one's own life and going into the world of the role to understand the rhythm required for the role is a process of self-transformation. This new understanding brought forth by this study's findings is significant because understanding the rhythm would help the actor to know what is required of them while on stage. A perfect example is seen where one has the role of playing on a specific day, one needs to understand all that is required, such as, the role to play, time to get up and go to bed, things to do, places to go, the way to talk with people, the mood of the character, and their breathing rhythm. When observing the change, the performer has made after days or years of practice, one will find the power produced is significant. The researcher believes this new understanding is crucial to the study and teaching of acting, as it would promote efficiency when acting thus portraying how the performer can put on a good show.

Challenges for Acting and Attributes for Improvement

Acting occurs in a physical world of events making it hard to fully understand such experiences from a psychological standpoint. An exclusive mainstream psychological approach to the transpersonal can never be sufficient in acting. Sometimes, such approaches may appear unnecessary. An integral comprehensive approach to the interpersonal needs a multi-perspective approach to the knowledge required in the supplementation of transpersonal psychology in this field and others. Another challenge is that transpersonal psychology is beyond only the rational and scientific when it comes to acting, because it includes the unmeasurable benefits of direct experience. This may result in products of undisciplined thinking by a team of extravagant spiritual-oriented professionals. In this case, actors need to use a rational approach to enhance cognition and magical thinking to avoid negative roles in this field. Three themes (discussed below) discovered by this research study are the basis of what makes actors perform well and create an association with the role.

1. Through establishing the broadness of acting and its equivalent governing factors, it is easy to relate the factors with transpersonal psychological factors that are required to be embraced for a better performance. This can be achievable by embracing transpersonal psychology through being ritualistic and reaching out to external thoughts within the scope of the topic.

2. The failure to embrace the ideology of transpersonal psychology leads to acting failure whereby an actor is unable to coordinate the mind and the general body behavior. The case is evident, especially when an actor resumes negative roles of the character. The mind needs to have a spiritual and holistic coordination with

other muscles in the body, blood pressure, and facial expressions to control the emotions that can attempt to show up at the face of the actor during performance. This study shows that if the transcendent is embraced fully, the actor successfully plays the role without the audience knowledge. Strict adherence to transpersonal psychologically inspired guidelines on acting can easily eliminate the challenges of acting brought about by emotions, voluntary muscles trembling, and blood pressure. The actor needs to appeal to the teachings of transpersonal psychology earned in theatre school to avoid challenges that are encountered during performance. Appealing to the spiritual and inner interests of the audience can help to achieve the intended goal of the performance easily as the audience mind will be set fully to follow the performance and actor's behavior should be under control.

3. Transpersonal psychology helps the actor to have the connection to the audience, internal factors, and to the role he/she is required to perform. Actors who have self-knowledge and mastered character and identity find acting easy. Transpersonal psychology promotes the fluid nature of acting. Study participants highlighted various factors impacting actors directly during acting include deep feelings for life events. In this case, transpersonal psychology assists actors with real-life events during acting. Therefore, the ability to feel passion, love, and frustrations, or any other real-life events

is vital in acting. Also, it helps to enlighten the society on the religious norms and how to deal with the economic and social challenges that the community face in their daily lives. Acting reflects the various ways of society lifestyle by depicting the old, new and the future expected changes in the community.

However, the most important aspect related to acting is the transpersonal psychological ideas which are involved in all themes. Spirituality, transformation, and expanded consciousness help the actor have the connection to the audience, internal factors, and to the role they are required to perform. The connection facilitated herein, gives the actor an upper hand to impact positively on the experience of the audience by tackling the topics that appear to trouble the society. Transpersonal psychology enables the actor to understand what the audiences need to hear from him at a certain time or circumstance. By closely studying the mood and the attitude of the audience, it is possible to decide the type of performance that will satisfy the audience in the form of entertainment.

A new role allows an actor to develop a deep sense of psychology of the people around him. He understands the people, their behaviors, accesses their mental approach, and then absorbs himself in the character in such an amazing way that is in complete synchronization with his audience. Hence, transpersonally, the audience learns from the actor and the actor learns from himself. In doing so, the actor solves the problems that were surrounding the people through a mastery of their intentions and their behavioral response towards the performance.

Acting as the Existence Beyond Self Through Transformation

Transformation can be backed by transpersonal psychological processes that enable the actor to embrace interpersonal psychology that mainly addresses human self-transformation. The development of consciousness, spiritual evolution, and crisis leads to crucial transformations that are beyond the Self. Actors need to borrow from their personal experiences to build true emotions and connect them with the character. Spiritual consciousness will be transcendent to the audience by the actor self-interpersonal psychology in embodying a character that advocates for the betterment of society through spiritual change.

Transpersonal psychology can assist actors in the creation of an enhanced self-consciousness while contributing to their spiritual development. For example, the ability to control one's emotions is great and transcending the self-concept is vital. Actors use their bodies as vehicles to the beings of their characters (roles) to achieve swift consciousness to their characters. With this process, actors access a higher hierarchy of consciousness to reflect their being, which produces higher understanding to their meaning of lives—their characters and their own. This process proves how the actors make mind-body-spiritual transformation thought acting. This study therefore claims that transpersonal method and theory is a necessary sub-structure for any such "higher" or growth acting. When actors embody roles, they become the carriers of the roles, and they suddenly need to know the lifespan of the role and experience the lifetime of the role. Another benefit of witnessing the character's life course and experience of life is that the actors themselves have gained some inspiration for their own life, their souls have been sublimated, and their bodies have also gone through transformation. Therefore, the audience will more likely be in sync with the actor's emotions. An actor's lifestyle lives affects their experience and determines both role playing and role switching. For the actor to transform people, according to this study, interpreting people and understanding their deeper thoughts about life is achievable through extensive acting experience. Life transformation requires the actor to understand empathy and the role completion either good or bad has an impact on the psychological expression of correct, rich, and accurate.

The first stage of acting is to discover the different elements of the inner personality. Having ample understanding of oneself requires more knowledge on the contents of waking of transformation and consciousness. This inner journey requires one to explore the reality unknown to one's psyche. This can be enhanced through a transpersonal transformation, which is exploring and studying ordinary personality and going beyond its further reaches. This will include applying psychological method designs such as meditation, self-hypnosis, automatic writing, and active imagination. It will open channels of communication with a higher consciousness where the transpersonal higher Self resides. In this way, individuals will discover unknown abilities, latent psychic knowledge, and express themselves in the most effective way—all crucial skills for effective acting.

Acting as the Subconscious Expression of Physiology

Transpersonal philosophy of mind is the understanding, but in our language, understanding means feeling, feeling means returning to the Self and a closure. The understanding required by an actor is quite different from what a scholar or critic needs. If the result of scientific analysis is thought, then the result of an actor's understanding should be a return to the Self. We can say that the post-analysis understanding is the development of self-regression.

Actors create characters through understanding, constantly feeling and experiencing, and as a result, continually deepen their understanding of the characters. The interpersonal understanding recognizes the interdependence of a person's mind and the existence of superior inner knowledge in psi-related experiences, dreams, and states of creative inspiration. As this study has sought to argue, transpersonal psychology is a fitting theoretical framework for actor training given the facts that transpersonal psychology values the diversity of expressions of human experience while recognizing the universality of its deeper dimensions, and actively seeks out and integrates insights on human nature and healing from a wide variety of cultures while recognizing the role of the cultural context in the experience of individuals and groups.

Self-transformation enables actors to integrate and connect with characters/roles. Transpersonal psychology acts as a bridge between two worlds of experiences. One is the ordinary and familiar world of experience of which is studied by mainstream psychologists and is consciously known. The other world of experience is also referred to as the hallucination experience which serves as a channel of and medium of experiences such as past life experience, lucid dreaming, psi-related experiences, and mystical experiences. Such experiences are said to evade the notice of most mainstream psychologists.

In the factors that aid role integration, the transcendence of actors requires excellent role and character integration. For actors to transcend the self in roles, high sensory memory is required. Transpersonal psychology assists actors to go beyond the Self through enhancing memorization, fluidity in switching roles, and many other crucial acting techniques. Also, a change in attitude by incorporating transpersonal perspectives into the practice, generates a deeper understanding of how sensory memory works, and with understanding, in turn, sensory memory can help actors achieve daily life activities that constitute acting while off stage. Furthermore, transpersonal psychology solves a problem that a person is not oneself in acting through phenomenological theory which elaborates how one may have experienced some of the aspects that later fails to leave an individual and ends up affecting our body, mind, as well as our consciousness in real life.

Regardless of the differences between actors and roles, actors must recognize, understand, and accept roles through their sensory memory, and integrate with them, to achieve self-transcendence and create the image of the role with the memory content in the Self. Appearing in front of the audience, the result of this creation is a good solution to the contradiction between the two, forming a unity between actors and roles. Therefore, actors should do their best to recognize, understand and accept the role, so that they and the role become one: the formation of unity between actors and characters; at the same time, in the process of creating their roles, the actor does not lose themselves.

Future Research

It is natural for humans to interpret and learn from personal experiences, and, after some time, we start to understand them. That's why special attention should be paid to the notion of "lived" in the phenomenological term "lived personal experience," as it plays a significant role for understanding phenomenological reflection, meaning, analysis, and insights. We can learn and gain new understandings through participatory research, where the narrative of one's life will allow the researcher to get new understandings of that particular person and provide understandings to the researcher about his or her own world. Additional understanding is achieved by re-reading the researcher's own description, gaining new insights, and re-writing the description until producing a satisfactory description in obtaining answers.

Future research on the phenomenological inquiry into the meaning of acting can be used to develop some nonconvention types of training methods for acting, which can be explored in this field. Additionally, future research could focus on identifying and studying various levels of acting that have been changing over time. Furthermore, exploring the nature through which diversification and globalization have greatly contributed towards change in nature of acting. Future researchers could focus on phenomenological inquiry of how various attributes brought up by changing times and trends as a result of globalization. However, future researchers could elaborate more on whether an actor's acting abilities are influenced by the way they are brought up. There have been a lot of insights and less research that identifies whether such stimulations are true. As a result, for anyone undertaking research on acting, this topic would be great as it would help more researchers understand phenomenological inquiry into the meaning of acting. Nevertheless, future research could also aim to engage actors from ethnicities other than Chinese to provide contrasting work to this dissertation.

The centered transpersonal psychological Self is discovered, or better yet, uncovered, through the analysis of concrete experiences of ourselves and of others in the acting community, communicated through research conversations and analyzed reflexively according to phenomenological, hermeneutic, and transpersonal operational guidelines. Through this process, the researcher uncovered not only an external Self, but also by understanding and transforming himself, the centered Self that transcends the objective Self.

The Selves transform themselves from being an "isolated

Self" to a "holistic Self" that is connected not only to the script and character, but to the whole "life world." The more a performer can see how they can function naturally as a part of the life world, the more they will understand the relationship between the world and themselves, and the more the world itself will change.

Until—and unless—this transformation can take place, performers will not become conscious or know how to change this intuitive feeling of loneliness in their existence and being-ness as actors. A loneliness that is remedied only if they can lose themselves by becoming an acting Self that is fully interconnected to the life world.

References

Adler, S. (2000). *The art of acting*. Applause Theatre & Cinema Books.

Alli, A. (2009). *The 8-circuit brain*. Vertical Pool Publishing.

Allport, G. W. (1937). *Personality: A psychological interpretation*. Holt.

Anderson, R., & Braud, W. (2011). *Transforming self and others through research: Transpersonal research methods and skills for the human sciences and humanities*. SUNY Press.

Artaud, A. (1958). *The theatre and its double*. Grove Press.

Auden, W. H. (1976). *Collected poems*. Faber & Faber.

Barua, A. (2009). *Phenomenology of religion*. Lexington Books.

Bates, B. (1987). *The way of the actor*. Shambhala Publications.

Benner, D. G. (2011). *Soulful spirituality: Becoming fully alive and deeply human.* Brazos Press.

Bogart, A., & Landau, T. (2004). The viewpoints book: A practical guide to viewpoints and composition. Theatre Communications Group.

Braud, W., & Anderson, R. (1998). *Transpersonal research methods for social sciences*. SAGE Publications.

Brecht, B. (1964). *Brecht on theatre: The development of an aesthetic*. Suhrkamp.

Burgoyne, S., Poulin, S. K. A., & Rearden, S. K. A. (1999). The impact of acting on student actors: Boundary blurring, growth, and emotional distress. *Theatre Topics, 9*(2), 157–179. https://doi.org/ 10.1353/tt.1999.0011

Chekhov, M. (2003). *To the actor*. Routledge.

Colaizzi, P. (1978). Psychological research as a phenomenologist views it. In R. S. Valle & M. King (Eds.), *Existential phenomenological alternatives for psychology* (48–71). Open University Press.

Cunningham, P. (2015). *Chapter 5: Transpersonal learning and memory* [PDF]. https://www2.rivier.edu/faculty/pcunningham/Research/Chapter_5_Transpersonal_Learning_and_Memory.pdf

Da, A. (1991). *The dawn horse testament*. Dawn Horse Press.

Encyclopedia Britannica. (2016). *Stanislavsky system*. https://www.britannica.com/art/Stanislavsky-system

Ernest, K., & Ketcham, C. (1992). *The spirituality of imperfection*. Bantam Books.

Evans, M. (2009). *Movement training for the modern actor*. Routledge.

Fljiyan, M. L. (2008). *The essence of the Stanislavski system.* China Film Press.

Friedman, H. L., & Hartelius, G. (2015). *The Wiley-Blackwell handbook of transpersonal psychology*. Wiley-Blackwell.

Galliene, E. L. (1973). *The mystic in the theatre*. Southern Illinois University Press.

Giannotti, T. (1995). *The inspiration of acting: Aesthetics and the will to heal in the human spirit* (Accession Order No. 740428541)[Doctoral dissertation, California Institute of Integral Studies]. ProQuest Dissertations and Theses.

Gilbert, N. (2008). *Researching social life* (3rd ed.). Sage.

Giorgi, A. (1975). An application of phenomenological method in psychology. In A. Giorgi & E. Murray (Eds.), *Duquesne studies in phenomenological psychology* (pp. 82–103). Duquesne University.

Giorgi, A. (1985). *Phenomenology and psychological research.* Duquesne University Press.

Giorgi, A. (2006). Concerning variations in the application of the phenomenological method. The *Humanistic Psychologist, 34*(4), 305–319. https://doi.org/10.1207/s15473333thp3404_2

Goldstein, T. R. (2015, February 5). Mindfulness and acting. *Psychology Today.* https://www.psychologytoday.com/gb/blog/the-mind-stage/201502/mindfulness-and-acting

Grammatopoulos, I., & Reynolds, M. (2013). The experience of drama: Why do people become involved with it? A phenomenological investigation of individuals' involvement with drama and its meaning. *Applied Theatre Research, 1*(1), 107–124. https://doi.org/10.1386/atr.1.1.107_1

Grotowski, J. (2002). *Towards a poor theatre.* Routledge.

Hodge, A. (2000). *Twentieth century actor training.* Routledge.

Housen, A. (1992). Validating a measure of aesthetic development for museums and schools. *ILVS Review, 2*(2), 1–19. http://kora.matrix.msu.edu/files/31/173/1F-AD-30F-8-VSA-a0b116-a_5730.pdf

Husserl, E. (2001). *Logical investigations* (J. N. Findlay, Trans.) Routledge. (Original work published 1901)

Ihde, D. (1986). *Experimental phenomenology: An introduction.* SUNY Press.

Jaspers, K. (1968). *A dynamic psychology of religion.* Harper & Row.

Johnston, D. W. (2007). *Active metaphysics: Acting as manual philosophy or phenomenological interpretations of acting theory* [Master's thesis, University of Sydney]. https://ses.library.usyd.edu.au/bitstream/handle/2123/3984/DW-Johnston-2007-Thesis.pdf?sequence=1

Jung, C. (2009). *The red book*. W. W. Norton & Company.

Kapsali, M. (2013). Rethinking actor training: Training body, mind and ... ideological awareness. *Theatre, dance and performance training, 4*(1), 73–86. https://doi.org/10.1080/19443927.2012.719834

Laverty, S. M. (2003). Hermeneutic phenomenology and phenomenology: A comparison of historical and methodological considerations. *International Journal of Qualitative Methods,* 21–35. https://doi.org/10.1177/160940690300200303

Leabhart, T. (2007). *Etienne decroux*. Routledge.

Lecoq, J. (2001). *The moving body* (D. Bradby, Trans.). Routledge.

Metzner, R. (1989). States of consciousness and transpersonal psychology. In R. S. Valle & S. Halling (Eds.) *Existential-phenomenological perspectives in psychology: Exploring the breadth of human experience* (pp. 329–338). Springer.

Meyerhold, V. (1978). *Meyerhold on theatre* (E. Braun, Ed.). Bloomsbury Methuen Drama.

Montouri, A. (1998). *Creative inquiry: From instrumental knowledge to love of knowledge*. In J. Petrankar (Ed.), *Light of knowledge.* Dharma Publishing.

Moon, A. (2008). *Toward a contemplative theatre: Body and mind in art and pedagogy of pacific performance project* (Accession Order No. 89237844) [Doctoral Dissertation]. ProQuest Dissertations and Theses.

Moss, L. (2006). *The intent to live*. Bantam-Dell.

Moustakas, C. (1994). *Phenomenological research methods.* Sage.

Murphy, M. (1992). *The future of the body: Explorations into the further evolution of human nature*. Penguin Putnam.

Murphy, M., & White, R. A. (1995). *In the zone: Transcendent experience in sports*. Penguin Books.

Myers, D. (2008). *Exploring psychology* (7th ed.). Worth.

Neff, M. P. (2005). *Aesthetic exploration and refinement: A computational framework for expressive character animation* [Doctoral dissertation, University of Toronto].

Porter, L. (1996). *Using drama therapy to explore emotional expression in actors: Implications for actor training programs* (Accession Order No. 740405451) [Master's thesis, California Institute of Integral Studies]. ProQuest Dissertations and Theses.

Powell, J. L., & Gilbert, T. (2006). Performativity and helping professions: Social theory, power and practice. *International Journal of Social Welfare, 16*(3), 193–201. https://doi.org/10.1111/j.1468-2397.2006.00459.x

Salata, K. (2007). *Directing the unwritten: The legacy of Grotowski* (Accession Order No. 304809792) [Doctoral dissertation, Stanford University]. ProQuest Dissertations and Theses.

Sarath, E. W. (2013). *Improvisation, creativity, and consciousness: Jazz as integral template for music, education, and society.* State University of New York Press.

Scotton, B. W. (1996). The contribution of C. G. Jung to transpersonal psychology. In B. W. Scotton, A. B. Chinen, & J. R. Battista (Eds.), *Textbook of transpersonal psychiatry and psychology* (pp. 39–51). Basic Books.

Seton, M. C. (2008). Post-dramatic stress: Negotiating vulnerability in performance. In I. Maxwell (Ed.) *Being there: After-proceedings of the 2006*

Conference on the Australian Association for Drama, Theatre and Performance studies. http://ses.library.usyd.edu.au/handle/2123/2518

Shevtsova, M. (2014). Stanislavsky to Grotowski: Actor to performer/doer. *New Theatre Quarterly, 30*(4), 333–340. https://doi.org/10.1017/s0266464x14000670

Shu, Q. (1982). *Theatre papers collection*. China Drama Publishing House.

Stanislavski, C. (2013). *An actor prepares* (E. R. Hapgood, Trans.). A & C Black. (Original work published 1936)

Stanislavski, C. (2014). *Creating a role* (E. R. Hapgood, Trans.). Bloomsbury Publishing. (Original work published 1957)

Stewart, D., & Mickunas, A. (1990). *Exploring phenomenology: Guide to field & its literature*. Ohio University Press.

Suzuki, T. (1986). *The way of the actor*. Theatre Communications Group.

Tart, C. T. (1969). *Altered states of consciousness: A book of readings*. Wiley.

Turner, V. (2001). *From ritual to theatre*. PAJ Publications.

Van Kaam, A. (1966). *Existential foundations of psychology*. Duquesne University Press.

van Manen, M. (2014). *Phenomenology of practice: Meaning-giving methods in phenomenological research and writing*. Routledge.

Wain, A. (2005). *Acting and essence: Experiencing essence, presence and archetype in the acting traditions of Stanislavski and Copeau* [Doctoral dissertation, University of Sydney]. Western Sydney University. http://handle.uws.edu.au:8081/1959.7/489652

Walsh, R., & Vaughan, F. (1993). On transpersonal definitions. *Journal of Transpersonal Psychology, 25*(2), 199–207.

Wilber, K. (2000). *Integral psychology*. Shambhala Publications.

Wilber, K. (2004). *The simple feeling of being: Embracing your true nature*. Shambhala Publications.

Wilber, K. (2007). *Integral spirituality*. Shambhala Publications.

Wylie-Marques, K. (2003). Opening the actor's spiritual heart: The Zen influence on Nô training and performance with notes on Stanislavski and the actor's spirituality. *Journal of Dramatic Theory and Criticism, 18*(1), 131–161.

Zarrilli, P. (2001). Negotiating performance epistemologies: Knowledges 'about,' 'in,' and 'for.' *Studies in Theatre and Performance, 21*(1), 31–46. https://doi.org/ 10.1386/stap.21.1.31

Zarrilli, P. B. (2004). Toward a phenomenological model of the actor's embodied modes of experience. *Theatre Journal, 56*(4), 653–666. https://doi.org/ 10.1353/tj.2004.0189

Zarrilli, P. B. (2007). An enactive approach to understanding acting. *Theatre Journal, 59*(4), 635–647. https://doi.org/ 10.1353/tj.2008.0002

Zehavi, G. (1999). *Integrating drama therapy back into the theatre: Providing a theoretical and a practical base for a two-year process with actors in training* (Accession Order No. 732071301) [Master's thesis, California Institute of Integral Studies]. ProQuest Doctoral Dissertations and Theses.

Appendix A: Invitation Letter

Dear NAME,

This letter is to invite you to take part in a conversation about your experience and thoughts regarding the meaning of acting.

You have been selected for your long-term practice and leadership in the field, as performer, director, or teacher; for the unique insights and perspectives you might offer about the past, present, and future development in drama, film, or television. Possible topics to explore in our conversation could include:

1. What is acting?

2. How important is technique and training?

3. Evaluate the training process.

4. Discuss the essential skills that make an actor.

5. How do you reconcile the acting role and the self? What defines an actor's identity? Can the actor-identity be separated from the individual-identity? Can stage-life be separated from real-life?

6. Describe important moments and experiences in your career.

7. What changes have occurred and else needs to change?

8. What is in the future of the acting field?

9. How can we promote the development of the drama, film, and television performance industry?

10. In your opinion, what are the reasons and significance of the transformation of drama, film, and television performance industry?

11. In the context of comprehensive transformation, what kind of special environment are you in? What are the advantages and disadvantages?

12. Over the past decades, your reform in the drama, film and television performance industry has achieved remarkable results. During this period, what are your personal measures? After the reform, what are your significant changes? What do you think of your achievements? Which aspects need to be strengthened?

13. Because you are an experienced director/actor, how does acting/directing influence your personal life? Through drama performance, what changes and help do you personally have to look at the problem?

14. Which of the actors you direct or work with that made an impression on you? And what effect does the drama show have on them? Is there any use in his life through theatrical performance?

15. In the process of continuing to strengthen support for the development of drama, film and television performance methods, you have personally implemented the strategy of what to do and what not to do. In which areas do you insist on doing something, and in which areas do you not do something?

16. In the performances, you guide or participate in, are there any ways to quickly adjust yourself and let yourself organically transform to achieve the purpose of accurately interpreting the characters?

17. Do you think that the existence of theatrical performance can surpass the transformation of self-behavior? (If so, what kind of transformation will this transformation of self-transcendence

bring to life?)

18. In the performances you participated in the past, did you participate in social service practice service performances? (If so, when? Where? What type of performance?)

19. Which of these social activities you participated in through theatrical performances are fresher in your memory? And what is the impact of your performance on the participants or the audience?

20. Do you think the art of theatrical performance is helpful for social development? (If so, what?) What impact does this help have on life?

21. Are there children attending or participating in the performance? (If so, when? Where? What type of performance?)

22. Do you think that the performance of theatrical performance is helpful for the future development of children's education? (If so, what?) What changes will be made to the development of children's education through the form of theatrical performance art?

I have drafted the above questions personally. I hope to have the opportunity to converse with you about the above topics. If you agree to participate, our conversation will take place via phone or Zoom at a mutually agreed-upon date and time. I look forward to receiving your reply indicating that you accept this invitation. Thank you for considering my request in your busy schedule. I wish you a smooth job and a happy life!

Sincerely,

Jiawei Liu

Appendix B: Participants' Backgrounds

Ren Chengwei (actor)

Ren Chengwei was born on May 3, 1970, in Hulin City, Chixi City, Heilongjiang Province, China. He graduated from the Shanghai Academy of Drama in 1993. In 1994, he first appeared in the TV series *The emperor flower*. In 2001, he starred in *Snow without traces* and won the 19th China Television Golden Eagle Award for audience favorite actor. In 2006, he co-starred in the TV series *Sha Jiaxuan* with Xu Qing, Chen Daoming, and Liu Jinshan. In 2011, he starred in Chuhan. In 2013, he starred in the TV series *The matchmaker*.

Li Jiahang (actor)

Li Jiahang, born on March 8, 1987, in Anshan City, Liaoning Province, China is a Chinese mainland actor. He graduated from the Shanghai Academy of Drama in 2010 with an undergraduate degree in performance. In 2008, he made his screen debut starring in the TV series *Golden Warrior* and in 2011 received attention for starring in the TV series *Love Apartment Season 2*. He has been in several TV series, including *New Jugger* (2011), *My Family Has Joy* (2012), *Amy Refuels* (2012), *Love Apartment Season 4* (2014), *The Legend* 骘 (2014), *The legend of Deng Shu* (2014), and *Newlywed apartment* (2015). He has also been in drama films including *The long song line of Xiu Lijiangshan* (2013), *Surgical winds and clouds* (2016), *Sky hunt* (2017), *Reading the heart* (2018), and *The huntsman* (2020).

Lei Guohua (director)

Lei Guohua is the national first-level director of Shanghai Dramatic Arts Center, the creative director of "Lei Guohua's director creative studio" of Shanghai Dramatic Arts Center, an exchange scholar of San Francisco University, a Chinese drama culture expert, an artistic director of Shanghai Performers Association Art Troupe, a member of the Shanghai Theatre Art Committee, and a member of the Directors Committee of the Chinese Drama Association and the Chinese Drama Association. He has served as the senior creative director of the American multinational group TVSN, the chief director of the Shanghai People's Art Theatre, and the director of the Nanjing Military Region Frontline Drama Troupe. He has nearly 40 years of experience in acting, director, screenwriter, and producer.

He has directed, planned, and produced nearly 100 theater performances and large-scale international cultural festivals and series of performances, including drama, opera, musicals, and children's dramas. He has won several awards for his directing including the Wenhua Award, the Five-One Project Award, and the Golden Lion Award—the highest award for Chinese drama culture. He has been invited to Hong Kong, Germany, the United States, and other countries for directors' creation, lectures, and cultural exchanges which have all been extremely successful.

Lin Hongtong (director)

A Chinese film writer, director, and performance teacher born in Fuzhou, Fujian province, China in 1938. After graduating from the Performance Department of Beijing Film Academy in 1960, he taught there as a teacher and has been engaged in film teaching for 35 years. He has served as a member in the council of Film Academy, a member of the Academic Committee, the vice president of China Film Society of Performing Arts, the director and art consultant of the Youth Film Studio. He has written 11 scripts and directed five films, television shows, and dramas. His screenplays have won several awards including the 1984 Government Outstanding Film Award, the Honor Award at the 13th Varna International Film Festival in 1986, and many others. He is author of several theoretical monographs including *The charm of movie actors*, *Skills and means for screen*, *The course of screen beauty*, and *The art of film performance.*

Li Yike (actor)

An actor from mainland China who graduated from the Performance Department of Shanghai Theatre Academy in 2010. In the same year, he was fortunate to be recognized by the famous director Kang Honglei and played Li Huolian in his large-scale revolutionary epic TV series *Nos annees francaises*. After that, he participated in the inspirational play *Massage*, the anti-war drama *The legendary sniper*, and the period play *Ji Hongchang* directed by Kang Honglei. In September 2016, he played the role of Cha Kun in the legendary drama *Nothing gold can stay*, directed by Ding Hei and starring Sun Li and Chen Xiao. In 2017, he played the role Ma Hanyuan in the military themed play *The king of land battle* directed by Kang Honglei. And in 2018, he participated in TV series *Face to sea*, directed by Yu Ding as a gift to China on its 40th anniversary of the reform.

Mi Zeng (Professor)

Associate Professor, graduated from the Department of Performance, Shanghai Academy of Drama. He served as the director of the performance teaching and research department of the performance department, the deputy secretary of the general branch of the performance department, and the deputy director of the performance department. He was awarded the outstanding art teacher in Shanghai, the outstanding member in the Education System of Shanghai, and other honors. He has published several papers including "How to mobilize students' enthusiasm for learning in performance teaching", "How actors read scripts", "emotional and emotional training," and "animal simulation training." He is the director of multi-act dramas including *Open your veil* and *Inside the field*.

Tian Lei (actor)

A Chinese actor of film and television born in Harbin, Heilongjiang Province, China on March 28, 1986 and a graduate of the Performance Department of The Central Academy of Drama. In 2008, he played a role in the drama *Strange Interlude* and officially entered the entertainment. In 2010, he was the backup singer and guest performer of Akino›s *Live in Beijing concert*. In 2012, he starred in the movie *Mr. Donkey*. In 2013, he starred in his first TV series *Bosom friend*. In 2014, he played the leading role of Wang Xijie in the urban love comedy *Don't let the people who love you wait too long*. In 2015, he starred in the urban emotional play *Three dads*. In the same year, he launched his first song "Growing with you." In 2016, he starred in the urban inspirational play *Women must be independent*.

Dr. Sean Wang Yang (director)

Theater Director, Acting Teacher, Shanghai Theatre Academy Acting Department teacher, Shanghai Dramatic Center director, and Beijing Film Production Company CHUAN program manager. Sean is a professional theater director. He has extensive experience in theater performance. He also teaches directing and acting, both of which he practices professionally. A central focus of his work is the Shakespeare theatre and contemporary dance. Sean has published several papers on directing and teaching. Dr. Wang is a sought after speaker of invited talks, workshops, and presentations around the world.

Yi Na (actor)

Yina is a Chinese mainland actress born on August 26, 1990 in Zibo, Shandong Province, China. She has appeared in *Xiangjiang North*, *Love Apartment 2*, and the micro-movie *Stranger next to the city image*.

Zhang Xiaoming (actor)

Chinese National First-Class, Plum Blossom Award-winning actress, graduate tutor, and member of the Chinese Dramatists Association, the Shanghai Dramatists Association, and the Shanghai TV Artists Association. She is a graduate of the Performance Department of Shanghai Theatre Academy. In 1982, she was an actress at the Shanghai People's Art Theatre; in 1995, she was an actress at the Shanghai Dramatic Arts Center; in 2000, she taught at the Performance Department of the Shanghai Theatre Academy. She is also a member of the Shanghai Branch of the Chinese Drama Association and a member of the Shanghai Branch of the China Television Association. She has won the Performance Individual Award at the first "Baogang Elegant Art," the Best Supporting Role Award at "Zuolin Drama Art," and published the work *The collection of fragment teaching on drama performance.*

www.ingramcontent.com/pod-product-compliance
Lightning Source LLC
Chambersburg PA
CBHW031145260225
22586CB00032B/269